"Don't be fooled by the pink nail polish.

Danica takes your hand and it's like a truck driver.

That's the yin and yang of Danica.

The exterior is nice and pretty—and underneath

she's as tough as steel."

— Bobby Rahal, team owner and 1986 Indy 500 winner, *People* Magazine

DANICA PATRICK

America's *Hottest* Racer

JONATHAN INGRAM & PAUL WEBB

Troy Lee Designs

MOTORBOOKS

First published in 2005 by Motorbooks, an imprint of MBI Publishing Company, Galtier Plaza, Suite 200, 380 Jackson Street, St. Paul, MN 55101-3885 USA

MBI Publishing Company titles are also available at discounts in bulk quantity for industrial or sales-promotional use. For details write to Special Sales Manager at MBI Publishing Company, Galtier Plaza, Suite 200, 380 Jackson Street, St. Paul, MN 55101-3885 USA

ISBN-13: 978-0-7603-2517-9
ISBN-10: 0-7603-2517-0

Acquisitions Editor: Lee Klancher
Associate Editor: Leah Noel
Designer: Mandy Iverson

Printed in The United States of America

On the cover:
Danica Patrick, 2005 Indianapolis 500 rookie of the year.
Getty Images

On the back cover:
With her combination of talent and good looks, Danica has become America's next sports hero.

Unless credited otherwise, photographs within are from Paul Webb's collection.

102644

CONTENTS

AN EXCEPTIONAL TALENT

by LYN ST. JAMES

Many talented race car drivers aspire to have a career in racing, many more than ever get the opportunity to succeed. In my opinion, you need to be exceptional in every area (talent, skill, personality, media savvy, technical ability, desire, physical and mental strength, determination, and even luck, just to name a few) to get the opportunity. Danica Patrick is exceptional, which is the primary reason she's gotten the opportunities she has, and has then delivered results along the way.

I met Danica when she attended my driver development program when she was 14. It became obvious to me that she was special. And the fact that her whole family was completely involved and supportive of her career aspirations just solidified my interest in helping her achieve her potential.

Her record in karting, along with her serious desire to reach the top levels of the sport, provided the foundation for potential success. The ingredients were all there.

I felt comfortable introducing Danica to leaders in the sport with the intention of getting them to step up and provide her with the resources and opportunities she needed to succeed. At times it seemed hopeless; people were always pleased and impressed to meet her, but they just didn't demonstrate any desire to DO anything.

Then Dan Davis, director of Ford Racing, took an interest and supported her in going to England to race Formula Fords. We all felt that going to the U.K. to race a junior formula would place Danica in the most competitive environment and prepare her for open-wheel professional racing, which was her goal. She excelled over there against incredible odds and her finish in the Formula Ford Festival was just extraordinary.

Danica's results just didn't seem to capture the attention of team owners until Bobby Rahal saw her run while he was heading up the Jaguar Formula 1 team in the U.K. I'm just so pleased that Bobby did exactly what I was trying to get a team owner to do: sign her up, integrate her into the team dynamics, and bring her up through the ranks based on her results. It's a shame that most team owners still just want instant success and avoid investing in talent development. The term "driver development" wasn't even in the vocabulary of race teams until recently. Fortunately that's changed, and that single change should provide more opportunities for talented, upcoming drivers who are properly prepared to excel.

When the subject of "women in racing" comes up, it's usually not something women in racing want to discuss. We just want to race and be who we are, but every woman who has been successful in racing (Shirley Muldowney, Janet Guthrie, Shawna Robinson, Sarah Fisher, and myself, to name just a few) have to deal with that label as best we can. I've always said the car doesn't know the difference, so let's start there. The real chal-lenge is how everyone on the team deals with a woman driver because it's always going to be the "**team**" that wins, not just the driver. But the media seem to focus on the driver and generally get tired of hearing all the thanks drivers want to give the team.

I'm now able to take a broader look at the subject and am excited about the future of women in racing. Young girls represent a significant number of racers in go-karts, soap box derby events, quarter midgets, micro midgets, and other grassroots forms of racing. And they're not just racing—they're winning. Moms and dads are now saying it's okay for their daughters to do what has always been okay for their sons to do. So with this significant increase in young girls winning races and with role models like Danica, I believe we'll see the sport grow its fan base and sponsor support to enable more women to get to the winner's circle at the top levels. It's all about opportunity and results. The stop-watch doesn't lie or take favorites; so grab your seats and hang on for an exciting time in racing.

Lyn St. James, 1992 Indianapolis 500 rookie of the year, seven-time Indy 500 starter, and 15 Indy car racer starts (www.lynstjames.com) ◇

MANIC FOR DANICA

by JONATHAN INGRAM

You have to be fast to earn the respect of the Indy faithful. Year after year, more than 350,000 devotees pack the stands to worship at America's altar of speed.

Cars hit speeds in excess of 240 miles per hour on the legendary circuit, and winning drivers once were showered with the media attention typically reserved for Olympic champions and Super Bowl MVPs. But this great racing spectacle faded in popularity in the 1990s—the result of racing organization turf wars that split the sport into two separate race series and left some of America's best-known drivers sitting on the sidelines during the race.

After 10 years of political warfare, the Indy 500's reputation had faded and, by 2005, the Indy 500 needed a new hero to move the event back toward America's center stage. The event found its catalyst when a young driver stepped into the limelight and performed with enough guts, nerve, and speed to attract the attention of even Indy's most skeptical fans. They had never seen an entrance quite like the one made by Danica Sue Patrick.

On a cool Sunday in May, Patrick roared into Turn One on the first of her four qualifying laps. She had been the fastest driver at the speedway on four of the seven practice days. Not only was this was a bit unusual for a rookie, but it was unheard of in the history of women competitors at the Indy 500. She went as deeply as anybody had dared into the left-hand, 90-degree turn, which Al Unser Jr. once said was like "driving down the barrel of a loaded shotgun." Whether it was tires not yet up to proper temperature, a loose chassis, a slight miscue at the turn-in point, or perhaps a left front wheel that scudded across the painted white line marking the apron, Patrick overcooked the corner. When the rear of her Honda-powered chassis stepped out and began to skate toward the wall, the professionals watching from the south end of pit road cringed and awaited the crash.

The cringe turned to horror as Patrick tried to correct the car for her big moment instead of lifting off the accelerator and accepting the inevitable spin into the wall. Nobody ever saves a car this out of shape, this sideways at Indy, especially in Turn One at 200 miles per hour.

"If you lift, you're going to spin and back into the wall," said one veteran engineer working for a rival team. "That's the safest thing you can do in that situation. If you keep

>> DANICA IN DEMAND

Even before the Indy 500, even as far away as Japan, Danica was in demand. Here she is consoled by Bobby Rahal after being bumped from the pole at her fourth IRL event, at Twin Ring Motegi, the state-of-the-art oval in Japan. *Michael Kim, USA LAT Photographic*

your foot in it and you correct too much, you can go straight into the wall. It's very, very dangerous."

Yet Danica kept her foot in it and corrected in tiny increments, freeze-framing time in a manner only the world's best athletes can manage. The chassis chattered as the tires regained their grip and her car made it through the turn, stunning the veterans on pit road and fans in the stands. Then she ran faster laps on each of her succeeding three circuits during the qualifying run, the last one at an average of 227.860 miles per hour.

All of this action was captured on live Sunday afternoon TV, making a wide audience realize a new driver had to be reckoned with—a 23-year-old, 5-foot–2-inch tall rookie who weighed 100 pounds and sometimes sported bright pink fingernail polish.

Danica Patrick had arrived.

In the two-week buildup to the race after qualifying, ABC Sports decided Danica's rookie performance was *the* story at Indy. She quickly became the speedway's biggest happening since the defending Formula 1 world champion Nigel Mansell arrived at Indy in 1993. Some insiders at the network argued they were putting too many eggs in one basket by making the race's only woman the centerpiece of the pre-race promotion. If she left the race early, they fretted, so would the viewers. On the other hand, if not for Danica, many viewers would not be watching the race at all.

>> GETTING HER BIG SHOT

Danica took her chance to run the 2005 Indy 500 very seriously, knowing it's a place that can make or break careers. When Danica ended up fourth on the grid, everyone was buzzing about the newest star in racing.

When the race finally got underway, all eyes, of course, were on this brassy rookie. When she made a stunning late-race pass for the lead in Turn One, the crowd erupted into "one of the loudest cheers in the history of the speedway," according to the track's vice president of communications Fred Nation, a veteran of four decades at the world's most famous race.

Was all this Danica mania just hype from those wanting to promote Indy racing? Not according to independent newspaper editors across the country. Details of Patrick's race exploits in the 500, where she ultimately finished fourth, appeared on the front page in 46 of the nation's 50 largest papers, and the TV ratings for the Indy 500 reached their highest level in a decade.

This was a whole new realm for the Greatest Spectacle in Racing. The British invasion created just as much collective excitement in American motorsports back in the 1960s, when British Formula 1 drivers and their spindly rear-engined cars took the Indy 500 by storm much like the Beatles took over American music. Andy Granatelli's turbine-powered swooshmobile was a big novelty hit later in that decade. But this was different, more than just racing.

"Dishy Dani" blared a headline in the *New York Daily News* as Patrick quickly got on a first-name basis with an entire nation. Soon enough, *Time*, *Sports Illustrated*, and *People* magazines called. *The New York Times* dedicated regular coverage to open-wheel racing for the first time in decades, its appeal suddenly resurrected from the bygone days of the Vanderbilt Cup races on Long Island. And some of the toughest judges in the sports writing world, the ever-cynical, always-critical veteran columnists, joyfully embraced all things Danica.

Television came calling, too. Danica appeared on ESPN's *SportsCenter*, *The Today Show*, and CNN to talk about her big Indy debut. David Letterman, co-owner of Patrick's team and the host of *The Late Show*, also brought his driver in for a guest appearance. Letterman's rival and certified car nut, Jay Leno, called from Los Angeles and asked Danica to come on *The Tonight Show*, too. No thanks, he was told. Even Herbie the Love Bug had his Disney people call to invite Danica to see the premiere of *Herbie: Fully Loaded*. And then Danica graced the red carpet again for the ESPY awards.

On the track, Patrick backed it up, as they say in racing, winning three poles in Indy Racing League events that summer, showing the sort of driving skill that turns up oh-so-rarely. She often out-qualified and sometimes out-raced her veteran teammates, including the previous year's Indy 500 winner Buddy Rice, as well as a hot crop of rookie-of-the-year contenders with far more experience in 800-horsepower cars. Along with a cascade of dark hair and a pretty face, the 23-year-old unleashed drop-dead intensity and molten fire from ebony eyes every time the helmet came off.

Around dinner tables, fathers learned from their teenage daughters about a new American role model. Karting facilities all over the country suddenly had a bumper crop of 10-year-old girls zinging around with the boys. This driver was changing the face of American sports, not just motor racing.

On May 15, 2005, in a gutsy move in a dangerous sport, America's newest sports hero had arrived. ◇

CHAPTER ONE

CLIMBING
THE PYRAMID

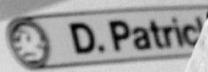

"[Danica] has desire, good judgment, and composure under pressure. And she has that thing that only champions have, that chip on the shoulder that says, You don't think I can do it? Come out and take a shot at me."

— Bobby Rahal, *Sports Illustrated*

When she was a young girl, Danica Patrick was fond of saying, "I'm going to win the Indy 500."

Her schoolgirl dreams were nurtured in a home where racing was part of the family and life progressed at full throttle. Her mother Bev and father T.J. met at a snowmobile race and were married shortly after. Within a year, Danica was born.

Danica's younger sister Brooke first took an interest in kart racing. But after several spins, Brooke's enthusiasm quickly faded and then 10-year-old Danica gave it a try. Danica quickly discovered she shared her father's full-throttle passion for driving. She threw all her efforts into karting. By age 12, Danica was winning regional World Karting Association (WKA) titles.

Her success is widely credited to the fact that the Patrick family made Danica's racing career a team effort. The family lived in Roscoe, Illinois, and traveled to the races together on the weekends. The Patricks' constant presence at the track made them one of the best-known foursomes in kart racing. T.J. led the team and helped fill out the budget, up to $60,000 per year, that wasn't covered by karting manufacturer sponsorships. Bev handled recording lap times and younger sister Brooke, who had led the family to karting, completed the cheerleading team.

Danica did her part and drove uncompromisingly hard.

"If you went into a corner side-by-side, she wasn't going to give," said Bruce Walls, a journalist who regularly covered WKA events. "She was fair but tough."

Patrick often drove for factory teams, which meant she had the best equipment, plus engine tuning and chassis setup assistance.

She drove high-strung race karts equipped with two-stroke motorcycle racing engines. Passing was difficult on the relatively short asphalt road circuits, so Danica needed to qualify well in order to finish up front—and

>> STANDARD BEARER

Before getting a chance behind the wheel of a Formula Ford, Danica had a strong record in the karting world. Here she holds the U.S. flag during the opening ceremonies of the 1997 World Karting Association/George Kugler Grand Nationals. As one of its most prominent graduates, Danica later became a standard bearer for the WKA. *WKA/Susan Taylor-Walls*

>> DREAMING BIG   (PAGES 12–13)

Danica Patrick poses with her Formula Ford shortly before a morning test in November 1998. With three years of hard work in entry-level cars ahead, she was determined to make her racing dreams come true. *Sutton Images*

>> SIGN OF THE TIMES
Many young girls identified with Patrick's
unintimidating size as well as her big
accomplishments during her days of WKA
competition, making her a fan favorite early
on. She was signing autographs long before
fans mobbed her at Indianapolis Motor
Speedway. *WKA/Susan Taylor-Walls*

she did just that. She claimed two of the prestigious
WKA Manufacturer's Cup championships and won 39 of
49 feature events in her class at age 14.

Patrick's talent and equipment put her head and
shoulders above most of her competitors in the WKA
junior ranks and on the same footing as future Indy
Racing League (IRL) champion Sam Hornish Jr. and
future NASCAR Busch Series champion Brian Vickers.

"Danica beat Sam Hornish a lot more often in karting
than she did in her rookie year in the Indy Racing
League," WKA President Randy Kugler said.

Hornish, three years older, once beat 12-year-old Patrick
in one of those side-by-side duels and she responded
later in the same race by wrecking him intentionally.

Patrick's intense desire to compete showed up again
at a Charlotte race in 1997. At age 15, Patrick had

>> LEADER OF THE PACK
Spending a final full season in the Junior class at age 15 resulted in two Grand National championships
for Danica. Her biggest year in karting came at age 14, when she won 39 of 49 feature events and won
two WKA Manufacturer's Cup national championships. *WKA/Bruce C. Walls*

>> BEATING THE BOYS

Patrick's smile at the top step of the podium tells the story at G&J Kartway in Camden, Ohio. The outcome would be very different at a Formula A race at the Lowe's Motor Speedway in Charlotte later that year. *WKA/Susan Taylor-Walls*

>> AT THE TOP OF HER GAME

Danica left her competition behind at the North American Karting Championships. Her winning ways meant no shortage of sponsorship opportunities, which helped pay bills that could run as high as $60,000 per year. *WKA/Bruce C. Walls*

stepped up to Formula A to race on board a new, more sophisticated kart. When she lost a nose cone from her kart and fell a lap behind the race leaders at Charlotte (in her class, Formula A, drivers who fall a lap behind the leader have to leave the race), the race officials waved the black flag at Danica, indicating she needed to leave the raceway. Danica defied the officials and refused to exit the race.

"When she finally came flying into the pits, she darn near ran over the president of the WKA," said Walls.

The passionate Patrick was immediately disqualified and later that day apologized to Kugler.

"She had tears in her eyes and said she wanted to prove she was faster than the guys in Formula A," said Kugler.

That same determination still runs deep in this driver who wants to be known not as a great woman driver, but as a great driver, period.

Instead of moving up to the senior class the next season at age 16, Patrick and her family decided to look into Formula Ford competition as the next step in her racing education.

THE RIGHT MOVES

Part of Danica's path to the top of the racing pyramid included enrolling in the Lyn St. James Foundation Driver Development Program at age 14. A seven-time Indy 500 competitor, St. James launched the program in the midst of her own career to help young women succeed in a male-dominated sport.

The foundation puts selected drivers through tests in a variety of cars "to try to get them out of their comfort zone, to see how they respond," said St. James. The barrage of tests measure physical and neurological responses and help drivers assess their weaknesses and strengths. Tips on physical training and guidance on writing bios and sponsor proposals conclude the two-day program, which is held annually in Indianapolis.

"We try to show them what to expect, but it's up to individuals for anything beyond that," says St. James, who was impressed early on by Patrick's poise and confidence.

Danica made it a point to get to know St. James, keeping in contact with her after participating in the program and developing a mentor relationship with her. In fact, only three months after they met in 1997, they attended an IRL race together in Orlando.

A few months later, when ABC Sports decided to run a profile of young elite female athletes, St. James recommended Patrick, who appeared in the documentary with future Olympic champion Tara Lipinski and tennis player Anna Kournikova. Years later, the none-too-shy Patrick cited the program as a turning point in becoming confident working with the media. The experience also reflected an already established aspect of her racing efforts.

"So much of Danica's success story is about her family," St. James says. "They traveled together all the time and really enjoyed each other's company. During the ABC program, it was clear that Danica was much more normal for her age than the other two athletes."

Patrick attended the Indy 500 with St. James for the first time in 1997 and returned a second time with her in 1998. Each time they visited the suite of the Mecom family of Texas during the race weekend. John Mecom III had already taken an avid interest in Danica's career, just as his father before him had done with quite a few race car drivers, and Mecom eventually pledged financial support.

Next, St. James convinced Dan Davis, director of Ford's worldwide racing program, to help Patrick. That's how the financing was established for Danica to follow a time-honored path to England, where she would learn her trade behind the wheel of a Formula Ford. For 25 years, this had been the starting point for any open-wheel driver who felt greatness beckoned.

continued on page 20

>> DANICA 101

AGE:
23

BIRTHPLACE:
Beloit, Wisconsin

RAISED:
Roscoe, Illinois

CURRENT RESIDENCE:
Phoenix, Arizona

MARITAL STATUS:
Engaged (wedding planned for November 2005)

RACING HEROES:
"No heroes, just role models."

GREATEST INFLUENCES:
"My parents."

IF SHE WASN'T A RACE CAR DRIVER:
"I've never had to think about it."

PHILOSOPHY:
"Life is what you make of it."

WEAKNESS:
Procrastination

FAVORITE CAR:
Ferrari 360

GREATEST AGGRAVATION:
"When people ask me about racing trying to be social. Only ask if you really want to know something."

Source: Rahal Letterman Racing

>> LEAVING THE NEST

Patrick competed in a more limited karting schedule in 1998, preparing for her move from her home in Roscoe, Illinois, to England. Here she hoists an eagle trophy that is significant of a Grand National victory at South Bend Raceway in Indiana. *Susan Taylor-Walls*

>> A NATURAL

Patrick's first sponsorship in Formula Fords came from a well-known racing photography agency, Sutton Images, a natural combination. This studio shot was taken five years before the ballyhooed session with *FHM* magazine. *Sutton Images*

>> THE EYES HAVE IT

The focus that would become one of her trademarks was evident at Danica's first race in the
Formula Vauxhall Junior Winter Series at the Croft circuit in England, her first competition in a car.
Sutton Images

There were mixed feelings when Danica left her home and family for the first time.

"When I was at the airport, my parents and my sister started to get choked up," Patrick recalled.

Always an emotional and supportive cheerleader for his first-born child, her father T. J. summed up the moment: "I can't imagine you not going and not having this opportunity. Go get 'em."

THE FORMULA FORD FESTIVAL

No matter how much a driver loves racing, the pyramid a driver has to climb to reach the top has such a steep incline that most who start at the bottom in Formula Fords never get a major league ride and give up.

"As far as racing up through the ranks, if you don't have the complete passion and dedication, you won't be able to go through the difficult times," Patrick said. "I just wanted to do it so badly; I wanted to make it to the top."

Patrick initially resided at the home of friends of the Mecom family in central England, the fertile crescent for the world's motor racing technology and home to a majority of Formula 1 teams. More importantly to Patrick, the manufacturing of the light, agile Formula Fords took place in England. She joined a number of young drivers who bring money or sponsorship to these factory teams in search of competitive equipment. The price for this opportunity in a factory ride can run as high as $150,000 annually for 20 races, plus the cost of seat time in testing. Often, these

>> TESTING, TESTING

One of the benefits of being on a factory team is the amount of testing and setup alteration a driver gets to do. Manufacturers constantly develop their cars because of the competitive market. The cars in Formula Fords handled like single seaters, but had no wings. Their top speed was 120 miles per hour under power from four-cylinder engines. *Sutton Images*

factory drivers' money merely keeps the lower echelon of England's racing industry in business. Yet enough of the aspiring drivers advance their careers to sustain the allure.

Patrick has bittersweet memories of the time she spent racing in various Formula Ford series.

"There were times that were tough on the soul," she said, "not being close to your family and friends."

She became part of an elite group of Formula Ford competitors who lived in the Milton Keynes area and drove for factory teams at Mygale or Van Diemen. Their age, distance from home, common passion for motor racing, and status as quick drivers formed a bond.

"We went through adolescence together," said American Pat Long, an international karting star. "We would carpool to the races and meet up sometimes afterward."

The group also included Scotsman Marino Franchitti, younger brother of IRL star Dario, and James Courtney, one of Australia's hottest prospects.

>> DANICA'S FAVORITE THINGS

HOBBIES:
Working out, traveling, nice dinners

CLOTHES:
Guys' briefs and a long-sleeve T-shirt

MUSIC:
Anything but country and classical

ALL-TIME FAVORITE CD:
***Jagged Little Pill*, Alanis Morissette**

TV SHOWS:
Sex and the City*, anything on the Food Network, and *The Late Show with David Letterman

MOVIES:
Tommy Boy, Dumb and Dumber

ACTORS:
Adam Sandler and Jim Carrey

ACTRESS:
Nicole Kidman

FOOD:
Anything healthy, especially fish, vegetables, and fruit

DRINK:
Water

DAY OF THE YEAR:
First day of summer

Source: Rahal Letterman Racing

>> FINE FESTIVAL

At the world's biggest gathering of aspiring professional drivers, Patrick again became a leader of the pack by finishing second at Brands Hatch's annual bracket competition for Formula Fords. It was a race that the Formula 1 industry closely followed and therefore was the reason future team owner Bobby Rahal found out about Danica. *Sutton Images*

Drivers sought out friends of a different experience level or who competed in different series to avoid any clashes on the track, which were frequent.

"I went over as a fair driver and I came back as a warrior," Long said. "You had to put the other guy in the dirt for position at any time, all the way back through the field."

The same was true for Danica, who flourished in the highly competitive environment.

"You can have a great day and be in the front," she said. "When you're having a bad day, you're 15 spots or more back."

Patrick gained a reputation among her peers for being extremely fast on given days but not always con-sistent in her pace from race to race, a description that fits many a well-known race car driver.

A few rare drivers follow a meteoric career path by regularly winning poles, races, and championships—or by showing well in the Formula Ford Festival at the storied Brands Hatch. Run under an elimination format with the best drivers in the world gathering for one year-end showdown, the Formula Ford Festival is one of the most-watched races of the year.

After two winless seasons in three different series, in the 2000 festival Patrick became the first American driver to ever finish as high as second.

No one in the racing industry seemed to notice, giving a cruel twist to Danica's accomplishment. One writer had referred to her as "gifted" in the Ford Festival, but that was a reference to the fact she advanced to second place when others ahead of her crashed out. She had shown pace, consistency, and made an aggressive move late in the race to gain second. As so often would be the case, Patrick had risen to the occasion.

Several months after her triumph in the Formula Ford Festival, Danica returned to the ranks of being an unheralded driver—wandering the garage at Indy Racing League events back in the United States with her racing bio in hand, looking for work during the early 2001 season before returning to England for another year of seasoning in Formula Ford. ◇

>> SKY HIGH

An 18-year-old Patrick hoists the trophy from her landmark result in the prestigious Formula Ford Festival at Brands Hatch, where she was the highest-finishing American ever. Below: Patrick's elation is evident as she joins winner Anthony Davidson of Britain and third-placed Robin Rudholm of Sweden on the podium. Davidson went on to Formula 3 the next season and Formula 1 testing, but Patrick found no takers in Europe. *Sutton Images*

"Women lose their history.

It was important to me to have

my little piece of it between hardcovers.

There were female hot-air balloonists, and later,

there were female race car drivers.

But that history is so easily forgotten.

It should not be because it creates a foundation

for the next generation."

— Janet Guthrie, on her book *A Life at Full Throttle*,
The New York Times

BRAVEHEARTS

Talk to any race car driver and you'll hear tales of perseverance, revenge, danger, deal-making, humor, and achievement. The stories they share are similar—whether the driver is a rookie, a seasoned veteran, a man, or a woman. In fact, when Michele Mouton was declared the winner at Pikes Peak in 1985, she wanted to know what all the fuss was about. "It's just another race," said the veteran World Rally Championship winner.

But when the driver is a woman, the other 55 are men, and the event has a long and storied tradition, well, people tend to make a fuss about it. And inevitably some men don't like it; men in the stands fans as well as those on the track.

So it goes for women who race professionally. They work hard and sacrifice to get their big-time breaks, or create them just like other racers do. They use their perseverance, skills, fortitude, and luck to win, and when they do, the general response is often one of surprise. It's not the most embracing welcome for a winner.

Nor is the place many of these successful women drivers end up in the history of motorsports—as a forgotten memory.

Only the diehard of diehard fans remember the post–World War II female drivers who first entered the competitive racing world—Louise Smith, Sara Christian, and Ethel Flock. A few more know the names of later heroes like Janet Guthrie, who rose to prominence in the late 1970s, followed by Patty Moise and Shawna Robinson.

Shirley Muldowney was the first American woman driver whose persistence, passion, and skill made it impossible for anyone to consider her a novelty act. "I was the only woman who ever wore the pants in Top

>> FAST IN PINK (PAGES 24–25, 26, 27)
Shirley Muldowney established herself as the most accomplished professional woman driver with three Top Fuel championships. She posted 18 National event victories in the NHRA, was the No. 1 qualifier 13 times, and recorded the top speed 19 times. She's shown on pages 24-25 on the track for the final time in 2003 and at right celebrating with her crew. *Jon Asher*

>> COLORADO CONQUEST

When Michele Mouton won the Pikes Peak Hillclimb in 1985, starting line procedures upset the French woman, who decided she was being delayed because officials did not want her to have a chance to tackle the imposing mountain under good conditions. Her anger at the officials motivated her to a record time at the event, though. She finished the 14-mile run aboard her Audi Quattro S1 13 seconds ahead of second-place finisher Al Unser Jr.

Fuel," she said, reflecting on the three National Hot Rod Association championships she won in 1977, 1980, and 1981.

Muldowney began drag racing on the streets of Schenectady, New York, before getting behind the wheel of Top Gas dragsters built and tuned by her first husband, Jack Muldowney. She had to fight for the right to compete while working her way up the ranks

and became the first woman to win a professional title in motor racing by taking a Funny Car victory in 1971 at Rockingham, North Carolina. Her three NHRA championships in Top Fuel (the fastest class in drag racing's most popular sanctioning body) just added more impressive highlights to her career.

A movie that told the story of her life, *Heart Like a Wheel*, was released in 1983, and by the time she had

a devastating crash in 1984, Muldowney was drag racing's best-known driver. She had tallied 17 national event victories in Top Fuel by then and returned to racing after recovering from her injuries to take one more at the Heartland Nationals in 1989.

When it came to getting beat by a woman, the male drivers eventually "got over it," Muldowney said. She raced until 2003, recording the quickest pass and fastest top speed of her career in her final season at age 63, winning elimination rounds against those competing for the championship.

continued on page 31

>> TOUGH WOMAN

In 1984, Shirley Muldowney lost a tire from her Top Fuel dragster at the end of a run at the Sanair Raceway in Montreal, causing an accident so violent that it ripped her car to bits. The roll cage separated from the frame rails and engine after hitting an embankment, which launched the roll cage so far that rescue workers initially couldn't find Muldowney in the mud 300 feet away. After a long, painful recovery, Muldowney returned to racing for another 20 years of 300-plus-mile-per-hour drag race competition.

>> NASCAR PIONEERS

Tim Flock used to joke that his sister Ethel (above, left) was named after the blend of gasoline. But stock car drivers had to take women seriously when they were behind the wheel, especially Louise Smith (above, right). She won 38 races in the Modified category at tracks from New York to Alabama. *International Motorsports Hall of Fame Archives*

>> LELLA'S MARCH

Lella Lombardi held sixth-place in the Spanish Grand Prix in Barcelona's Montjuic Park in 1975 when officials halted the race after 26 laps because four bystanders were killed in an accident. Driving a March 751, she became the only woman to finish in the points in an F1 Grand Prix. *Sutton Images*

>> UNIQUE AURORA

South Africa's Desire Wilson gained fame as a winner in Britain's short-lived Aurora F1 series. Wilson took top honors in 1980 at Brands Hatch, albeit in a short field of just five entries. Wilson later co-drove a Ferrari 512 BB/LM with Janet Guthrie at Sebring in 1982. *Sutton Images*

>> QUEEN OF THE HILL

World Rally driver Michele Mouton first competed at Pikes Peak in 1984 in a Quattro designed for Group B in the World Rally Championship. The next year Mouton confessed she forgot one of the mountain's corners en route to victory. "My heart was beating so hard it was outside my body," she said. *Audi AG*

>> TAMING THE WILDCAT

In 1978, Janet Guthrie qualified at Indy in a Wildcat built by George Bignotti for road courses. She started 15th in the Cosworth-powered machine with a speed of 190.325 miles per hour and finished ninth, the best by a woman at Indy until Danica Patrick's fourth-place finish in 2005. *Indianapolis Motor Speedway*

"The thing I'm most proud of is that we hung in there for 33 years without ever having a major [sponsorship] deal," she said.

Women drivers have never had an easy path to racing success, often only getting support from those established team owners, drivers, mechanics, and officials willing to keep motor racing open to anybody with the guts to try it and courage stick with it. These proponents supporters have often been opposed by many critics, who sought reasons to sideline women drivers.

"If I had spun out on a restart at Indianapolis in 1977 and taken out two competitors, there wouldn't be a woman at Indianapolis to this day," said Guthrie.

Before the lack of sponsorship ended her brief 11-race career in Indy car racing, Guthrie's 1978 ninth-place finish at Indianapolis remained the only top 10 result by a woman until 2005—when Danica Patrick came in fourth. Guthrie's fifth-place result at Milwaukee in 1979 remained the best by a woman for 21 years.

In NASCAR racing, Guthrie gave Ricky Rudd some tough competition for rookie-of-the-year honors in 1977, despite intentional efforts by the sanctioning body to limit her practice time and otherwise make her feel unwelcome. NASCAR officials feared her success would discredit stock car racing by making it look too easy. As if to take revenge on NASCAR officials and their silly

notions, Guthrie's best finish in 33 starts came at Bristol, the most physically demanding NASCAR track. Her sixth-place result on the Tennessee track remains the highest finish by a woman driver in the modern super-speedway era of NASCAR's premier series.

NASCAR was not the only group upset by the entrance of women into racing—as Muldowney can

>> SEVEN TIMES AN INDY LADY

A driver and team need sponsorship dollars to run at Indy and Lyn St. James generated enough support for seven races. But it was not possible to land the same budgets as the front-runners. "What sponsors see in proposals and what they believe, I found, were often different," she said. *Indianapolis Motor Speedway*

>> GENETICS

In the final week of practice before the 89th running of the Indy 500, a reporter asked Danica Patrick if genetic differences could cause a man to be a better race car driver than a woman.

"Or," she replied, "a female driver to be a better race car driver than a man?"

attest to from the beer cans thrown at her early on in her career. Guthrie underwent hazing from fans at Indy, too, in the form of rude comments and signs in the grandstands.

Overlooking these detractors became part of the job, as did hearing comparisons to other women drivers.

Of course, that didn't mean the women drivers liked the situation. "They wanted and still want to be recognized and respected for their skills, not compared to other women drivers," said Lyn St. James, who competed in seven Indy 500s.

>> PRO BIKER

One of the most successful women competing at the professional level, Angelle Sampey took three straight NHRA Pro Stock Bike championships from 2000–2002. Below she races against U.S. Army teammate Antron Brown in 2005. *Jon Asher*

>> QUALIFYING HEROICS

When Janet Guthrie qualified for her first Indy 500 in 1977, she drove a Lightning chassis whose handling had been "spooky" much of the week in practice due to a lack of replacement parts after a crash and an undiscovered faulty steering box. Once those problems were fixed by her Rolla Vollstedt team, the engine began to slowly devour itself during the final practice. With time running out in the warmups, Guthrie depended on her knowledge about engines acquired through years of building her own to get her powerplant to survive.

In qualifying, her four flying laps averaged 188.403 miles per hour, the last ending with no oil pressure. Her average speed was 18th fastest in a 33-car field from an entry of 85 cars.

>> SWAN SONG

BAM, a new team owned by Beth Ann Morgenthau, offered a Winston Cup ride to Shawna Robinson in 2002. But the team had teething troubles and tried six drivers without success. Robinson's top performance in NASCAR came in 1994 when she won a Busch Series pole in Atlanta. *Nigel Kinrade*

Like Janet Guthrie, St. James took the road racing route to Indy, racing professionally in the Kelly American Challenge Series and then in the International Motor Sports Association's Camel GT, where she won four events, including a solo drive to victory at Watkins Glen.

St. James made women drivers a fact of life at the Indy 500 with her participation for six straight years, before returning for her seventh start in 2000. Her best result was 11th in her rookie year in 1992, which came amid a stellar class of newcomers. For that finish, she earned the 1992 rookie-of-the-year title (an honor won by Ms. Danica Patrick in 2005) and a warm reception at the awards' banquet.

While racing coverage usually has long been preoccupied by comparing women to women—as in the first female driver to do this, or the first to do that—Danica Patrick became the first female driver in top-level open-wheel racing who forced a comparison to the other

male drivers because her Indy speeds could not be ignored. And the roar that greeted her when she took the lead at the 2005 Indy 500 with 11 laps to go testified that the racing world is ready to cheer on a great woman driver.

"Because Danica's performance had been so extraordinary, I think there was a comfort level with the fans that hadn't been there before," St. James said.

But overcoming the hurdle of finding sponsorship is still difficult for young women drivers. Muldowney, Guthrie, St. James, and IRL-contender Sarah Fisher ran into concrete walls in the hunt for a major sponsorship.

"Certainly at the time I thought I had established a record that would enable me to continue in the sport," Guthrie said. "Professional sponsor-seekers assured me that it would be a piece of cake. Didn't happen. I drove only 11 Indy car races, spread over four years, yet it was

>> FAN FAVORITE

Voted the IRL's most popular driver for three straight years, Sarah Fisher was the first to eclipse Janet Guthrie's mark for highest finish by a woman in an Indy car with a third at the Kentucky Speedway in 2000. Her fourth-place start tied Guthrie's record set at Pocono in 1979. *Sutton/Swope*

In 1992, Lyn St. James qualified at Indy for the first time after switching to one of Dick Simon's backup chassis on the final day, becoming the oldest rookie to qualify for the event (she was 45). After negotiating permission from Ford, with whom she had an ongoing business relationship, St. James switched from an underpowered, older Cosworth to a Chevy engine to make the field. She finished 11th and won rookie-of-the-year honors while competing against future Champ Car champions Jimmy Vasser and Paul Tracy and three-time Formula 1 champion Nelson Piquet, who had a devastating, career-ending practice crash.

more than two decades before Sarah Fisher broke most of my records."

Fisher, a winner in midget and sprint car races as a teenager, rapidly advanced to the IRL, where she eventually started 48 races from 1999–2004. At age 21, she nearly won a 2001 IRL race versus Sam Hornish Jr. at Homestead, Florida, before finishing second in her second full season aboard the entries of respected team owner Derrick Walker. After switching to Dreyer & Reinbold Racing in 2002, Fisher won a pole and led two races for a total of 30 laps. By the 2004 season, however, her only start was at Indy.

In the absence of sponsorship, and like Guthrie before her, Fisher decided to try her luck in NASCAR, joining Richard Childress Racing in the new wave of driver development programs (following a diversity effort launched by the sanctioning body). The switch to NASCAR meant starting over on the short tracks of the minor leagues.

Drivers like Danica Patrick and rising stars Erin Crocker and Katherine Legge won't necessarily face the same challenges, though, as they have received more training in the lower ranks before moving up. "Very good car owners are taking care of them and putting them in good equipment," Fisher said.

>> FORCE TO RECKON WITH

A potential future star, Ashley Force seeks to follow her father's success. A 13-time Funny Car champion, John Force has chosen not to rush his daughter's career. Ashley competed in Top Alcohol Dragster in 2005 and veterans do not expect her in a Funny Car before 2007. *Jon Asher*

>> THE FAMILY CAR

When Louise Smith drove her husband's new Ford coupe to Daytona Beach in 1947 to watch the stock car races, she couldn't resist entering the event. Behind the wheel of the family car, Smith crashed in the race, and by time she returned home to Greensville, South Carolina, word was all over town thanks to a photo of her wrecked car in the newspaper. It was the first race in a career that lasted another nine years. Like Muldowney, she was eventually elected to the International Motorsports Hall of Fame at Talladega.

In 2005, Crocker began competing in the NASCAR Busch Series for Ray Evernham Motorsports and Legge became a winner as a rookie in the Toyota Atlantic Series while driving in a development program for PKV Racing, which also runs an elite team in the Champ Car series. Only Crocker has major sponsorship so far, hers coming from General Mills.

St. James has done a lot to change the situation for women drivers, launching the Invitational Driver Development Program through the Lyn St. James Foundation so qualified young girls can get a chance to see if racing is for them. Danica Patrick was one participant who not only became a professional driver, but landed lucrative sponsorships.

continued on page 40

>> WILL POWER

Hillary Will has posted victories in the Top Alcohol Dragster class and has ambitions to move up to the Top Fuel class in 2006. Her driving coach Paula Murphy (left) piloted everything from Funny Cars to rocket cars and land-speed record machines in the 1960s and 1970s. *Jon Asher*

>> CROCKER WATCH

Erin Crocker leads the way in NASCAR's diversity push. She has an engineering degree and a victory in the World of Outlaws sprint car series. Team owner Ray Evernham moved up his budding star to the Busch Series in 2005 in preparation for a fully sponsored season in 2006. *Nigel Kinrade (above)/Bob Costanzo and ARCA (below)*

>> LEGGE UP

Katherine Legge, shown above celebrating one of her Toyota Atlantic victories, drives for PKV Racing. The team plans to move her up to Champ Cars in 2007. Below, Liz Halliday, a show jumper on the equestrian circuit, co-drove to victory in the LMP2 class in the American Le Mans Series with Intersport Racing in 2005.

>> PRESSURE COOKER

The following excerpt is reprinted with permission from Janet Guthrie: A Life at Full Throttle, *copyright 2005, Sports Media Publishing, Inc. Guthrie wrote the first passage shortly after Arlene Hiss finished 14th in an Indy car race at Phoenix in March 1976. Hiss ran the race at a slow pace, and the racers reacted with an outpouring of ridicule and criticism. As the result of one poor outing, Hiss lost her sponsorship, and her race career essentially ended. Guthrie, in the meantime, was scheduled to race at Trenton, New Jersey, shortly after the Hiss debacle. As a result, members of the race community were trying to prevent Guthrie from racing at Trenton, as they were skeptical that the racetrack had room for female competitors. The following passage illustrates the difficult task that greeted women racers in the late 1970s.*

I remember a moment, on a grubby, oil-smeared propeller plane droning toward Milwaukee—weary of Bryant's and Toyota's tours, the endless smiles and photos; haunted by the knowledge that the least mishap at Trenton would precipitate a deluge of scorn and derision and end my racing forever—when I almost wished the plane would crash, so it would be over with.

The fuss wasn't really about me, of course. The fuss was about the cultural mindset as to what women could and should—or couldn't and shouldn't—attempt. The women's movement had made this opportunity, this chance of a lifetime, available to me. I was in the right place at the right time with the right background of experience, dedication, and passion. Having found myself, by historical accident, on the cutting edge of women's incursions into traditionally male fields, I had become the flash point, the lightning rod for the volatile emotions that festered in the aftermath of the legal successes of the women's movement.

The second passage takes place at the press conference for the Trenton race. At the conference, Guthrie faces hard questions from the press and tough criticism from the race community (in this case, legendary racer Bobby Unser).

Later as the affair wound down, a reporter for *The New York Times* beckoned from a phone booth, the receiver to his ear. He put his hand over the mouthpiece. "Bobby Unser," he said. "He just told me he could teach me how to drive better than you. I told him I didn't drive. He said he 'could take a hitch-hiker, give him a Corvette off a showroom floor, and turn him into a faster driver than her."

Bobby Unser had never seen me drive anything. It was too much . . . and it cracked me up. "A hitch-hiker!" I laughed. "You're kidding! He really is a male chauvinist pig, isn't he?"

All that made headlines on the front page of the Sunday *New York Times* sports section.

Finally, trailed by photographers and cameramen, we were outside—outside where my car, my Indy car, sat in its neat little package of a trailer, right there on Fifth Avenue. The splendors of the city stood all around: beyond the fountains, the fabled Plaza Hotel; Bergdorf Goodman, full of women in mink; A La Vielle Russie, with its Fabergé eggs in their original Cyrillic-lettered cases; Tiffany, where diamonds peeked coyly from heaps of sawdust in the windows. Central Park opened up on the right, and the horse-drawn carriages waited at the curb.

I felt like Alice gone through the looking glass.

Amid the Fifth Avenue cops and the curious, my crew opened up the trailer and there it was . . . Vollstedt's blue car, my car, reality. I hungered for it like a person starved.

At long last, we were on our way to Trenton.

"To me it's a mystery," said St. James of the difficulty finding sponsors for qualified women drivers.

St. James feels Danica has had success with sponsors, because she came into Indy racing under the umbrella of a front-line team with a strong financial base. Needing $3.5 million from a major sponsor to fund Danica's Indy car debut season, the Rahal Letterman Racing team let her take the Argent Mortgage sponsorship

>> YOUTH MOVEMENT

At the age of 11, Elena Myers became one of the hottest prospects in motorcycle racing with her victory at the Portland International Raceway in the 125cc class. After starting at age 8 on miniature motorcycles, she hopes to become a professional road racer for a major factory team. *Myers Family Collection (left)/Don Daugherty (below)*

that was already established during the 2004 IRL season with drivers Buddy Rice and Vitor Meira. For 2005, Meira switched to a new sponsorship deal from long-time racing participant John Menard and his chain of building supply warehouses.

Now that Danica's getting so much attention for her top-notch performances, more sponsors are coming out of the woodwork. So are those interested in getting more women into victory lane. "Not a day or a week goes by without getting an inquiry about my driver development program or an e-mail . . . about Danica's success," St. James said.

Some of those e-mails come from young girls, who admire how Danica refused to give up on her dream. While making an appearance in her home state of Illinois prior to the IRL's 15th race at Chicagoland Speedway, Danica made a trip to Sugar River Raceway. The track was the closest karting facility to her family's house in Roscoe, Illinois, and the place Danica first learned to drive. "I was surprised how many girls were out there," she said after the visit. "When they get out of their karts, the 10-year-old boys and girls were all patting each other on the back. I think that's so cool."

Very cool, indeed. ◇

>> FOR MORE READING

Shirley Muldowney, Lyn St. James, and Janet Guthrie have all written books about their groundbreaking careers. If you'd like to learn more about the history of women in racing, these three fascinating reads are a great place to start:

Janet Guthrie: A Life at Full Throttle
By Janet Guthrie
Sports Media Publishing, Inc. (2005)

The Ride of Your Life: A Race Car Driver's Journey
By Lyn St. James
Hyperion (2002)

Tales from the Track
By Shirley Muldowney and Bill Stephens
Sports Publishing LLC (2005)

"I need to beat them, belittle them, and make them feel small. Trying to run them off the road at 170 miles per hour isn't sweet and kind."

—Danica Patrick, on her feelings towards the competition,
FHM magazine

CHAPTER THREE

DRIVING
TO THE TOP

Hell rarely contains as much fury as Danica Patrick when her ability to drive a race car is scorned. This burning desire to prove herself eventually made a believer of Bobby Rahal, who directed Jaguar's Formula 1 team in England during the final season Patrick raced Formula Fords in 2001.

"When she took the opportunity to go to England to race, that showed me a lot about her determination," Rahal said. "I know a lot of drivers who aren't willing to take that kind of chance to further their career."

During his nine-month stint in 2001 with Jaguar, Rahal was among the Formula 1 insiders aware of the diminutive young woman who was making big impressions with her speed in the development ranks. So was Bernie Ecclestone, director of Formula 1's business affairs, who sent a letter to Danica's parents about their rising star.

"Tell her not to give up—she will have to mix it up with the boys and fight harder for her position," wrote Ecclestone, the most powerful man in racing. "I hope everything works out for her."

Agents and team owners had contacted her as well. Advised to go see Patrick for himself by Lyn St. James when the two former Indy 500 competitors crossed paths at the Goodwood Festival, Rahal saw the American teenager in action at Oulton Park.

As fate turned out, neither Patrick nor the 1986 Indy 500 winner Rahal had the career success they anticipated during their stints in England. Patrick did not win a race in three seasons of Formula Ford and Rahal failed to turn around Jaguar's F1 fortune. Both returned to the United States to focus on other avenues in 2002, which eventually brought them together.

Danica kept her name in circulation by winning the Toyota Pro/Celebrity Race at Long Beach's glamorous street race, her first victory since karting. Rahal, meanwhile, was in the midst of plans to return his Ohio-based team to the Indy 500 for the first time since splitting from the event along with his fellow Champ Car team owners in 1995. Despite not having a sponsor for her, Rahal signed Patrick midway through 2002 to a three-year contract that was designed to bring her to the world's greatest race.

"I think she could be the first female driver to win the Indy 500," Rahal said.

Laboring in the seemingly dry vineyards of Formula Ford had paid off for Patrick. The deal that put a promising new talent under contract also paid off for Team Rahal, which landed Argent Mortgage and Norwalk Furniture as sponsors for Patrick in the Toyota Atlantic Series.

After a handful of warm-up races in the Barber Dodge Pro Series in the latter half of 2002, Patrick started her stint in the Atlantics in 2003 determined to prove her abilities as a driver. The first task would be to relieve her rivals of any illusions that she received an opportunity at Team Rahal due to her gender.

>> DOUBLING DOWN (PAGES 42-43)

With two races to go in the 2003 Atlantic season, Jon Fogarty became the Rahal team's second entry driver. Here he confers with Danica prior to the street race in Denver, where the defending champ finished fourth and Danica fifth. *TnT Photo*

>> STREET RACING

Shown here racing the streets of Toronto in July 2004, Danica was fast and aggressive in her second season of Toyota Atlantic competition. She briefly led the points and completed every lap.

"She forced the guys to give her respect," said David Empringham, a two-time Atlantic champion working as a driving coach to some of Patrick's chief competitors. "Her determination in cars that are physically difficult to drive was quite incredible. She was fortunate to get an opportunity. But she had a much tougher time because she was a female. There weren't a lot of guys who were ready to get beat by a woman."

Seven-time Atlantic race winner Calvin Fish, Danica's first driving instructor in the Atlantic cars, had a similar view.

"In every race situation, it seemed like Danica felt she had to make a statement—that she wasn't going to give any ground, that she was for real," Fish said.

At the opening round of the 2003 season on the streets of Monterrey, Mexico, she finished her first Atlantic race in third place. She became the first woman to stand on a post-race podium in the series' 31 seasons. But she kept her eye on bigger prizes and asserted herself with confidence.

"Everyone is always looking for the latest and greatest thing, but for me racing isn't about being the best female

>> RIDE SHOPPING

When seeking to start their professional career in the United States, Danica and one of her fellow Formula Ford competitors in England, Patrick Long (right), tested a BMW M3 at Sebring, Florida, in December 2001. Team owner Tom Milner provided the car, but ultimately American Le Mans Series rules did not allow it to compete. *Richard Dole/LAT Photographic*

driver in the sport, but being the best driver I can possibly be," she said. "I cringe sometimes when I hear people say that I'm the first female driver to do this or that. Don't get me wrong—I know that I fill a unique niche in racing, so I will use that to my advantage to benefit my sponsors. But I know I'll have made it when the media and the other drivers simply refer to me as a driver."

This shrewd approach put everyone on notice that Danica regarded herself as a competitor on the same footing as others, much like her responses on the track. This battle to establish herself came with the territory, and Danica willingly fought the constant uphill struggle

to be accepted on her terms on and off the track, where the double standard continued to rule.

Confrontations in the paddock are as much a part of racing as fighting for territory on the track. But Patrick's efforts to protect her turf were more difficult because of her gender.

"If Danica got in anybody's face to complain about their driving, the drivers would call her a bitch," said one longtime supplier to the series. "But they also made it very difficult for her on the track."

Occasionally, the team owner pitched in on the political front, emphasizing that Danica belonged.

>> CELEBRITY STATUS

Danica returned to the United States after racing in England to make an appearance at the Long Beach Toyota celebrity race. She qualified on the pole and led Tommy Kendall the entire way, ultimately ending up with a popular win and trip to victory lane with celebrity winner Dara Torres. This was Patrick's first victory in a car, but it came in a "tin top" instead of the open wheelers she had spent three years driving in England. *Lesley Ann Miller, LAT Photographic (below)*

"I saw a level of dedication that is uncommon in most drivers," Rahal said at the team's fourth race at Laguna Seca. "There are hundreds of kids who come along with talent, but they are not all willing to pay the price to be better. Danica had the talent, the will to sacrifice for her career, and the work ethic needed to develop her skill. I didn't see it as a gamble when I signed her. I saw it as a chance to give back to this sport that has been so good to me and to help develop a driver who, in my opinion, will be the next big thing in racing."

When it came to skill development, Patrick's toughest task was learning how to work with the team to set up her chassis for optimum performance.

"It took Danica a lot of time and a lot of laps to give feedback as to what the car was doing," her instructor Fish said, referring to her initial testing.

"I didn't learn a whole lot about the cars [in England]," acknowledged Patrick. "I think they told me to go drive whatever I had. They kind of took the fastest guy and used his setup."

>> SHIFTING GEARS

Danica landed a full-time job with Team Rahal midway in 2002. One of the advantages was tutelage from team owner Bobby Rahal, who goes over shifting points at Mid-Ohio prior to a test at the team's home track.

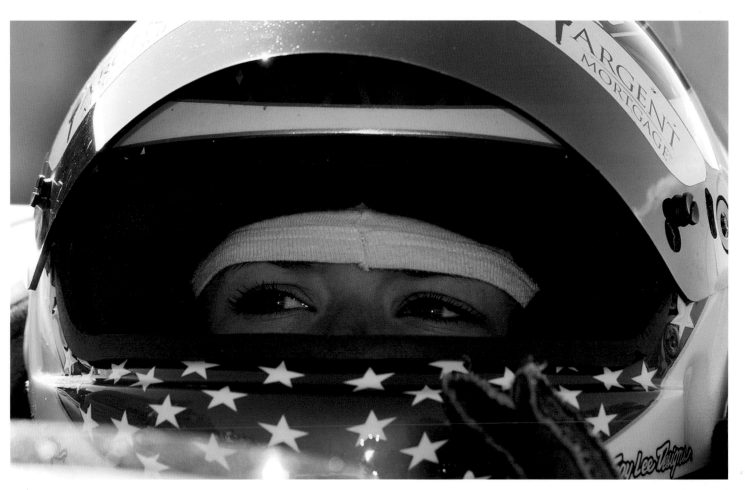

>> EYES WIDE OPEN
Danica relied on her own deep well of motivation, which proved an effective way to deal with the pressure of being a young woman competing in what was previously regarded as a young men's series.

Learning how to drive a car not perfectly attuned to one's own style is crucial for any driver. Over the course of a season, a car is hardly ever perfect in races or qualifying. In order to beat the talented young drivers in the Atlantic series, proper chassis setup and aerodynamic tuning were necessary. The same would be true if Danica wanted to step up to the Indy Racing League.

Falling short of the podium in the seven races after the opener in Mexico, Team Rahal decided to hire the 2002 series champion Jon Fogarty to help improve chassis setup in testing, then asked him to drive a second car in two races at season's end.

"We were different personalities," Fogarty said of his brief stint as Danica's teammate. "I'm very easygoing and

Danica externalizes her frustrations more. We worked through those issues. Technically, I was quicker to get the car up to speed, particularly in the high-speed turns. She had the database from the telemetry in our car, which showed her what I was doing."

Danica quickly got faster with car preparation input from her teammate and with help from the data showing Fogarty's degree of throttle applications or braking on the different portions of a circuit. After finishing second in the Miami season finale to Michael Valiante, two positions ahead of Fogarty, she ended where she had started—on the podium.

It had been an outstanding season, given that the Atlantics usually raced as a preliminary to the Champ Car

>> RACING 101
A PRIMER ON THE VARIETY OF OPEN-WHEEL RACING SERIES

FORMULA 1

Formula 1 (F1) is the world's premier motorsport. The F1 world championship series is comprised of 18 road racing events in 16 countries. The U.S. Grand Prix has been held at the Indianapolis Motor Speedway's combined infield and oval circuit since 2000. Technically the most sophisticated series and most expensive, annual budgets range as high as $350 million for factory-backed teams. The sport is as popular in European countries as football is in America, which is one reason Ferrari's superstar driver Michael Schumacher is one of the highest-paid athletes in the world.

INDY RACING LEAGUE

Founded by Tony George in 1996, the Indy Racing League (IRL) puts an emphasis on oval racing for Indy-type cars. George also wanted to bring control of U.S. open-wheel racing back under the direction of the Indianapolis Motor Speedway, owned by his family. To run a 17-race schedule with one car costs $5 million. Engine manufacturers, such as Honda, Toyota and Chevy, usually provide about $1.7 million per car for selected teams.

CHAMP CAR

The Champ Car Series started as CART, for Championship Auto Racing Teams. Organized in 1979 by Indy car team owners, CART ran road and street circuits, plus ovals. CART eventually declared bankruptcy due to high costs and because the Indy 500 fell off the schedule when the IRL started. Running all Lola cars with Ford Cosworth engines, the 13-race series has been revived as Champ Car under new ownership. Running a car in the series for a year costs about $4 million per year.

TOYOTA ATLANTIC

Since 1974, the Toyota Atlantic Series has featured intermediate single-seater cars. Due to less sophisticated cars and fewer events, the series maintained lower costs and is a logical stepping stone for young drivers. The series features 12 races in Canada, the United States, and Mexico. The cars use Swift chassis and four-cylinder Toyota engines. Running the Toyota Atlantic Series currently costs from $675,000 to $1 million per car, per year.

AMERICAN LE MANS SERIES (ALMS)

Launched in 1999, the American Le Mans Series uses the same rule book as the famed Le Mans 24-hour race and runs the same prototypes and production-based GT cars. The 10-race schedule is built around a break in June that allows teams to participate in the famous French race, which is not part of the U.S. championship. The cost varies according to the classes. A top-line prototype season costs $4 million annually, and an entry level GT car about $1.5 million.

ROLEX SPORTS CAR SERIES

The Rolex Sports Car Series features prototypes and GT cars similar to the ALMS, but with different rules governing engines and chassis eligibility. The France family, which owns NASCAR, organized the series in 2000. The 11-race endurance sports car series seeks to lower equipment costs so any competitor can have a chance at winning. Factory teams keep the costs of winning regularly at $3.5 million for prototypes and $1 million for GT.

WORLD KARTING ASSOCIATION (WKA)

The World Karting Association (WKA), based in Charlotte, North Carolina, offers a variety of karting classes organized according to type of kart, engine, power, and age group. The Junior category is for ages up to 15 years old and the Senior level begins at age 16. To win a national points championship, a driver would usually run a minimum of six major events in the Eastern United States, from Wisconsin to Daytona Beach, at an annual cost of $60,000.

>> STEPPING UP

Rahal entered Patrick in a handful of Barber Dodge Pro Series races in the second half of 2002 in preparation for the 2003 launch of the Toyota Atlantic team. It gave her a chance to adjust to the team and tracks like Mid-Ohio and Toronto.

races, where team owners were always on the lookout for new, unsigned talent in the lower ranks.

"The competition was vicious at times," Empringham said about the wheel-to-wheel blocking and fighting for position. Never one to give an inch, Danica completed 10 of the 12 races and finished sixth in the points, one position behind the highest rookie, Aaron Justus.

Entering the 2004 season, Patrick and her team, where karting graduate Chris Festa had been added as a full-time No. 2 driver, considered themselves a contender for victories and a championship. From Empringham's point of view, however, the Rahal team was third best on the grid. Pacific Coast and Sierra Sierra ranked ahead of Team Rahal when it came to engineering the series' Toyota-powered Swift cars. The 12-race season played out along these lines. Fogarty, driving for Pacific Coast, won six races and

the title. Scotsman Ryan Dalziel won four races for Sierra Sierra, taking second in the championship race after winning two races the year before.

Racking up a string of six top-five finishes, Danica earned her first pole and briefly led the points at mid-season. But in the final six races, she failed to make the podium. On three occasions, Danica displayed what was becoming a trademark ability to come back from adversity when multi-car incidents in the first corner damaged her car and dropped her to the rear. Each time, she catapulted back through the field, finishing third at Monterrey, seventh at Portland, and fourth at Vancouver.

Most remarkable was the comeback in the streets of Vancouver.

"There were cars everywhere on the start," Patrick said. "I got hit and was forced back outside. The next thing I knew a car came flying over the top of my car. It

>> FAST COMPANY

Danica talks with former Atlantic driver and Speed TV commentator Calvin Fish. He gave Patrick her first driving instruction after she signed up with Team Rahal for the Atlantic series.

was a crash fest. After that, my car was damaged and it was hard to hold it steady down the straight. I had to really adjust my driving style because if you drove the car too hard or too easy, it wouldn't respond." Ultimately, Patrick was the only driver to complete every lap of the season.

At times, it seemed Patrick never let off the accelerator. At Cleveland, after Alex Figge unintentionally rear-ended and spun his Pacific Coast teammate Fogarty near the end of the race, she sent a bottle of champagne to the duo's restaurant table that evening, complete with an obviously sarcastic note congratulating Figge on his day. At the previous race in Portland, where Patrick had won the pole and had been leading the points, she was the one sent spinning at the start by an ill-advised move from Figge.

Despite not gaining a victory and the constant questions in chat rooms at racing Web sites, Rahal was already gearing up for Danica's move to the Indy 500, especially after his driver Buddy Rice won the event in 2004.

"Danica has really made strides, and I think she can go to Indy and be competitive," he said at mid-season, shortly after Rice had won at Indy in a Honda-powered Panoz chassis. "I am serious about her being a factor. I have said all along that neither Danica nor Team Rahal is interested in going to Indy simply as a publicity stunt."

The team owner's comments made prior to the third race in her final Atlantic season caught Patrick a little by surprise.

"Running the Indy 500 is a dream of every young driver," she said. "The opportunity to go to Indy with a team that has won the biggest race in the world is incredible." ◇

>> SPEAKING OUT

Danica spent a lot of time with media, honing her speaking skills as much as her driving.

>> SI SEÑORITA

Patrick prepares for her first Toyota Atlantic race on the streets of Monterrey, Mexico, in 2003.

She became the first woman to finish on the podium in the series' 31-year history.

>> TITANIC TOYOTA ATLANTIC

The two years Danica Patrick spent in the Toyota Atlantic Series turned out to be landmark seasons for a series with a long history of producing professional drivers.

In 2003, A. J. Allmendinger tied a record first set by Gilles Villeneuve with nine poles for the RuSports team and won 7 of 12 races before moving up with his team to Champ Car. Luis Diaz, the winner of one pole that season, moved into the Target Chip Ganassi Racing sports car program in the Grand American Series, where Michael Valiante, a three-time winner in 2003, would also find driving opportunities.

In 2004, Ryan Dalziel followed two poles and two victories in his rookie campaign with five poles and four victories before moving on to the American Le Mans Series along with another Atlantic series winner from 2004, Alex Figge. Bryan Sellers, on the podium twice, also moved up to the ALMS.

Jon Fogarty returned to claim his second Atlantic championship in 2004, winning six poles and six races in 12 starts. At the end of the 2003 season, Bobby Rahal offered Fogarty the job of replacing injured driver Kenny Brack in the Indy Racing League. But road racer Fogarty decided he didn't want to compete on ovals, leaving the job open for 2000 Atlantic champion Buddy Rice, who won at Indy in 2004 with Rahal. For his part, Fogarty continued his road racing career in 2005 in the American Le Mans Series.

>> QUICK STUDY

After starting fifth, Patrick moved quickly into third on the Fundidora Parque circuit in Monterrey.

"She forced the guys to give her respect," two-time champion David Empringham said.

>> FUN AT FUNDIDORA

Race winner Michael Valiante (right), and runner-up Jonathan Macri (left), and Patrick celebrate their accomplishments on the Fundidora Parque street circuit. It would be the end of her first season before Danica returned to the podium in Miami.

>> NO LOOKING BACK

A year after she won the Toyota celebrity race as an aspiring driver looking for a job, Danica awaits the start of practice for the Toyota Atlantics at the Long Beach street circuit in April 2003.

>> LONG DAY AT THE BEACH

Danica didn't have her best outing at the well-known downtown street circuit of Long Beach in 2003.
Disappointed to qualify 10th, she finished 14th after being involved in a crash.

>> FULL CHAT

The Milwaukee Mile gave Danica her first outing on an oval. It was the only oval on the Toyota Atlantic schedule, since the series operated under the ownership of Champ Car, which was primarily focused on road circuits.

>> FHM CALLING

Shortly after her performance in the 2005 Indy 500, Danica Patrick became one of the most popular women on the web. Web sites carrying photos of her scantily-clad photo session in the pages of *FHM* magazine received an estimated 110 million hits. Some of the fly-by-night sites that allow users to download photos scanned from the magazine crashed because the demand was so high.

With her appearance in the April 2003 issue of the popular men's magazine, Danica might have done more than any other individual to publicize the 10-year-old Indy Racing League (IRL).

"It was an opportunity to find sponsorship and it opened lots of doors," Danica said in an interview with *Time* magazine. "You have to do what you have to do, within reason and in respect to yourself, but I don't feel one bit uncomfortable with it. I look at the pictures and I think, 'The girls are pretty.' I had fun."

>> SIGNING ON

All Toyota Atlantic drivers have to attend autograph sessions for the fans. Danica was as obliging as any other. Here, she signs a race tire (above) and a copy of her photo spread in *FHM* magazine (below). *TnT Photo*

Speed Dem
Formula race-car driver Danica
hottest thing on wheels since

>> FAMILY FOURTH

Danica and Bev, her mother, head for the pit lane for the start of practice at the Cleveland Burke
Lakefront Airport on July 4, 2003. Danica qualified 10th and finished fifth at the grueling, rough
airport circuit.

>> STILL SMILING

In a rookie season that started with a podium finish, top three results did not follow easily. But with three Toyota Atlantic races to go in the season, Danica was all smiles as the series moved to Montreal in August 2003.

>> DEUCES WILD

At the Montreal circuit where the casino reigns supreme, Patrick qualified fifth and ran seventh in the race on the Circuit Gilles Villeneuve. The team had started using Jon Fogarty to help with chassis setup in private testing.

>> PROUD PAIR

Bobby Rahal and Bev Patrick watch it all come together in Miami. Eleven races after finishing on the podium in Mexico, Danica returned to the stand in Miami, where she qualified fifth and finished second.

>> STREET RACER

Patrick took to the new street circuits of Denver and Miami quickly, where precision and shorter radius corners worked well for her. Also, other drivers had no experience on the courses, which were put up overnight and taken down by Monday.

>> FINE FINISH

Bobby Rahal and Danica were both thrilled with the results from the final race of the 2003 Toyota Atlantic Series. Danica ended the season as she began, with a hard fought podium position, this time in Miami.

>> TOUGH COMPETITIORS

The drivers who competed in the 2003 Toyota Atlantic season included the following: (from left, bottom row) Joey Hand, Danica Patrick, Michael Valiante, (second row) Romain Dumas, Aaron Justus, Eric Jensen, Luiz Diaz, A. J. Allmendinger, (third row) Alex Garcia, Kyle Krisiloff, Marc Devellis, Jonathan Macri, (back row) Eduardo Figueroa, Philip Fayer, and Ryan Dalziel. *TnT Photo*

>> NEW LOOK

Danica had come a long way from the days when Sparco helped sponsor her in the karting days. She looked forward to the 2004 Toyota Atlantic season with experience, a good team, and no lack of confidence.

>> CHECK IT OUT

Having arrived as a professional driver, Patrick receives her reward for a sixth-place finish in the final points standings in 2003. Rookie Aaron Justus finished 14 points ahead in fifth, tops among the newcomers. *TnT Photo*

>> CRASH COURSE

Bev Patrick cheers on her daughter as she makes her way back through the field at the 2004 Monterrey season opener. Danica enjoyed the fruits of her labor after an accident at the first corner. Comebacks would soon be a trademark.

>> HEAD GAME

On the weekend she took the points lead briefly and won her first pole, Danica confers with the crew in the paddock at the Portland track. She was spun at the first corner after a slow start following her pole, the first of her career.

>> ANOTHER FIRST

Danica wins her first pole and gets congratulations from longtime Rahal Letterman Racing chief mechanic Jim Prescott. It's another first for a female driver in the series.

>> TABLES TURNED

Patrick nipped former teammate Fogarty (right) by 4/100ths of a second to win her first pole at Portland International Raceway on June 19, 2004.

>> PAYING THE BILLS

With improved results and more exposure, Danica is even more popular at get-togethers with team sponsors. Here Danica talks to a group prior to racing at Portland.

>> NOT COOL

A dismal Danica thinks over an eighth-place run in qualifying on the wide-open runways of the
Burke Lakefront Airport in Cleveland.

>> DARK CLOUD

Vancouver started a string of races with mixed results. In practice, Danica was alone on the circuit prior to the challenging street race in western Canada.

>> CHANGING FORTUNES

After a dismal qualifying session, Danica has a great drive in the race to finish a closing third at Cleveland, the kind of driving team owners appreciate!

>> HEADS DOWN

Despite this bonzai move by Josh Hunt, Patrick survived the incident and finished an amazing fourth in Vancouver.

>> **STREET REPEAT**
Danica again found
the Denver circuit to
her liking, setting the
race's fastest lap.

>> **OUT OF HIS RANGE**
A spirited race-long battle with the talented Canadian Andrew Ranger resulted in a fourth-place
finish at Montreal, the second-to-last round of the 2004 season.

>> DRY LAKE AT LAGUNA

In the final race at the challenging road course at Laguna Seca, Danica qualified well in fourth, but faded to eighth in the race, uncharacteristic of her normally aggressive style. It would have been hard for anyone to predict on this day that less than 10 months later Danica would lead the Indy 500 and be on a *Sports Illustrated* cover.

On the check:

September 12, 2004

TOYOTA ATLANTIC — Toyota Atlantic

September 12, 2004

TOYOTA ATLANTIC — Toyota Atlantic
2004 Series, 3rd Place

Danica Patrick

Forty Seven Thousand and Nine Hundred Seventy Five — $47,975.00

>> CHECKING OUT

Danica receives the third-place championship trophy from Dick Eidswick of Champ Car and Les Unger of Toyota. In her final season of Atlantics, she was the only driver to finish every lap in the season, completing 800 miles. *Phillip Abbott/LAT Photographic*

"NASCAR isn't used to

being put on the third page of *USA Today*,

which means they'll probably be trying to hire

Danica away from us."

— Bobby Rahal, team owner, *Sports Illustrated*

CHAPTER FOUR

THE BOBBY & DAVE SHOW

Danica Patrick found success during her rookie year in the Indy Racing League driving for one of the best teams on the circuit—Rahal Letterman Racing. The team draws its character from Bobby Rahal, a rare breed of man who combines the guts and talent to win at the top levels in racing with the savvy to run successful businesses and race teams. It was no surprise Rahal won the Indy 500 as a team owner in 2004 with Buddy Rice behind the wheel, nearly two decades after driving to the checkers himself.

In 2005, the defending champions added a new driver to its lineup, one few expected to have such an astounding impact on the Indy 500.

Rahal initially signed Danica Patrick to a contract that started with a stint in Atlantic racing, but the ultimate goal was an Indy berth.

"Bobby showed a lot of faith in signing me to a three-year contract without a sponsor," Patrick said of the original deal struck midway in 2002.

At a time when the driver was shopping for rides in a variety of racing paddocks, only Rahal stepped up with a long-term agreement that put her behind the wheel at

the Brickyard in the month of May. Many racing observers thought the move was a gamble, but it paid off for the entire IRL as Danica's presence at Indy brought back some of the glory that used to surround the legendary race.

In fact, for the first time in years, the Indy 500 became the major sports story of the Memorial Day weekend, edging out coverage of NASCAR's Coca-Cola 600.

"The top fold of the *USA Today*, twice," Patrick said about the paper's coverage of the race. "I wasn't expecting that."

>> MAN WITH A PLAN (PAGES 74–75)
Bobby Rahal won 24 Champ Car races, 18 poles, three points championships, and the Indy 500 as a driver. He came back to the Indy 500 in 2005 as the defending winner once again, this time as the owner of Rahal Letterman Racing.

>> THINGS LOOKING UP
Famed comedian David Letterman won the 2004 race with driver Buddy Rice under the newly announced Rahal Letterman Racing banner and then had the hottest driver at the track, Danica Patrick, when the team returned for 2005.

>> WINNING FORMULA

Bobby Rahal won a race in each of the three seasons he competed in the Canadian-based Formula Atlantic Series from 1976–78. Shown here in Quebec City in 1978, Rahal was already cultivating a relationship with Jim Trueman, owner of Red Roof Inns and the "Sleep Cheap" slogan.

Perhaps Rahal was. He spent nine months in 2001 running the Jaguar Formula 1 team in England, where he witnessed two young rising stars of F1, Jenson Button and Kimi Raikkonen, jump straight from the ranks of the lower formula cars to front-line F1 teams. He also had front-row seats to the rapidly developing career of 20-year-old Fernando Alonso, destined to become F1's youngest champion. Perhaps it was time for him to take a chance on a young driver. And who was a better bet than a 20-year-old woman who knew her way around the track?

The business of signing Patrick midway in 2002 was risky. The team had not yet confirmed a sponsor for the Atlantic team at a cost of $1 million per year. Elsewhere,

for the first time Rahal was committing to full-time programs in both the Champ Car series with driver Michel Jourdain Jr. and the rival IRL with driver Kenny Brack for the upcoming campaign in 2003.

But Rahal knew an attractive, well-spoken young woman like Danica could attract sponsorship dollars. Shortly after her signing, the team announced backing from Norwalk Furniture and Argent Mortgage. Even when Patrick struggled midway in her first Toyota Atlantic season, Rahal kept the faith. "I don't see it as a gamble," he said.

"I know the opportunity to work with a championship-caliber team like Team Rahal is an incredible opportunity for a young driver," Patrick said. "What is even more

>> FORWARD MARCH

Rahal showed winning form early in his CART career, taking victories on both a road course and an oval in his rookie season of 1982. Here, Rahal leads the pack down the front straight at the Pocono International Raceway in 1983 aboard his Truesports March 83C Cosworth.

incredible is the opportunity to work with a champion like Bobby. He has a plan in mind that will advance my career at the right time."

Rahal, who eventually decided to hold Patrick back a second year in Atlantics, knew a lot about career timing. He worked hard at being in the right place at the right time in his early days, an era when a variety of options were presented to young drivers. Rahal started racing with the Sports Car Club of America (SCCA), which selected him for the prestigious honor of the President's Cup in 1975 after his winning performance in the Formula Atlantic category at the National Championship Runoffs. An award with a long history (it was first presented by President Dwight Eisenhower at the White House), the President's Cup launched Rahal's career.

"Getting the President's Cup was very special to me," said Rahal, whose father Michael raced at the club level before introducing his son to racing. "My parents were on hand, and it was the biggest award I'd received at that point. It certainly brought us recognition, and I think a lot came out of it in the end."

At age 23, Rahal moved to the professional version of the Atlantic series, where he raced against future F1 champion Keke Rosberg and the legendary Gilles Villeneuve and won a race in each of the 1976, 1977, and 1978 seasons. Following those two drivers to Europe, Rahal raced Formula 3 and Formula 2, securing an offer from team owner Walter Wolf to drive in the U.S. and Canadian Grands Prix.

Keeping his options open, Rahal raced in the Canadian-American series, whose high-horsepower

Legendary announcer Tom Carnegie interviews 30-year-old Bobby Rahal at the Indianapolis 500 in May 1983. In Beloit, Wisconsin, T. J. and Bev Patrick were taking care of their infant daughter Danica. Rahal started sixth in that year's 500 and finished 20th due to a broken radiator.

prototypes were very popular in North America, and he pursued endurance racing events at Le Mans and Daytona. Co-driving to victory in the 24 Hours of Daytona in 1981 aboard a Porsche 935 Turbo finally brought him the acclaim he had been seeking. The following year, Rahal entered the Championship Auto Racing Teams (CART) series driving for a fellow Ohioan, entrepreneur and Red Roof Inn motel chain founder Jim Trueman.

A lifelong road racer and backer of Rahal's 1981 Daytona effort, Trueman became Rahal's mentor. Both were attracted to the CART series that had split from the Indy 500 and the United States Auto Club (USAC) in

>> ONE FOR JIM

Bobby Rahal's victory in the 1986 Indy 500 came both a little late and just in the nick of time. In a year when the race was postponed twice for rain, the 70th Indy 500 started six days late and on a Saturday. But when the 350,000 fans returned a second weekend to see the event, they were treated to one of the greatest races in Indy history.

Rahal was well-liked and highly respected, yet had never won at Indy. He also was driving for former driver Jim Trueman, who was battling cancer, making Rahal the emotional favorite for a victory.

It seemed like a sign from above when the caution lights went on with five laps to go in the race. Moments before, Kevin Cogan appeared to have the race won. After leading on five occasions and for 55 laps, Rahal had just been passed by Cogan, with only 13 more laps to go. As those drivers rode in first and second, the tension mounted prior to the final restart when two green flag laps were remaining.

In one of the most famous exchanges in live sports television, leader Cogan declined to answer any questions from the ABC Sports crew as the field followed behind the safety car.

"I'm kind of busy right now, Sam," he told broadcaster Sam Posey.

Rick Mears, riding in third place, had the best seat in the house.

"Bobby was just ready at the right time and made a great move," he later said. "That's what makes a champion." Rahal drafted past Cogan on the front straight, diving underneath in Turn One as the crowd let out a thunderous cheer.

"I said to myself, 'Man, now go. If you're ever going to drive two laps as fast as you can, now is the time,'" Rahal said.

By the final lap, Rahal knew he would not be overtaken again.

"I looked in my mirrors, saw I had a pretty good lead, and started yelling," he said.

When he stepped out of the car, he brimmed with emotion.

"This one is for Jim Trueman," he said over the public address system and for television microphones. "I think everybody knows I love him, and this is the one thing I can give him. If anything can repay him for all the things he's done for me over the years, maybe this can."

For his part, a brave Trueman was appreciative.

"I asked Bobby to do the best he could, and I think he drove the best race of his life," he said after the win.

Rahal had done so in the nick of time. Eleven days after the victory lane celebration, Trueman lost his battle with cancer and died.

>> HAIL FROM THE CHIEF

New Zealander Steve Horne formed a crucial link in the Truesports team's triumvirate. Here, the chief mechanic salutes his driver rolling down pit road en route to an emotional winner's celebration at the 1986 Indy 500. Eleven days later, team founder Jim Trueman died of cancer. *Dan R. Boyd*

>> NEW WAVE

The future of Indy car racing takes over the podium at the Phoenix International Raceway in 1984, where winner Rahal is flanked by a pair of 22-year-olds. Michael Andretti (left) eventually joined Rahal in the ranks of team ownership. Al Unser Jr. later won the Indy 500 twice.

>> RED ROOFED AT THE FINISH

Rahal counted five street course victories among his total. Here, he covers the curbs at the Surfer's Paradise street course on the Gold Coast of Australia just prior to his final race in California in 1998. Rehal retained the white helmet with the "red roof" design throughout his CART career.

1979 to pursue an independent schedule including both road races and ovals. But the centerpiece of the CART schedule remained the Indy 500, still under USAC sanction. Even for those enamored with road racing on twisty circuits that turn left and right, the Indy oval had always been the hallowed ground of speed.

It became the best of all worlds for Rahal, who learned about business from Trueman, pursued his first love of road racing, and learned the oval trade as preparation for Indy, where the Truesports team won in its fifth entry in 1986. Three years after Trueman's death, Rahal changed teams, then launched a team with Carl Hogan in 1992. That year, Rahal became the first owner/driver in CART history to win the championship. After splitting with Hogan in 1996, Team Rahal came into existence in part through his a longtime friendship

with comedian and TV star David Letterman, which started when Rahal appeared on *Late Night with David Letterman* following his Indy 500 triumph.

Before his driving career ended in 1998, Rahal had established himself in the CART record books in virtually every category. He won 24 races, 18 poles, and more than $16 million in purse money en route to three championships, two with Truesports in 1986 and 1987. He recorded three more victories after his Daytona triumph in the Camel GT series, including one at the legendary 12 Hours of Sebring in a Porsche 962 and a solo win on a street circuit in Columbus, Ohio. He also drove BMW, Corvette and Ford Mustang prototypes.

With this background and experience, Rahal provided knowledgeable leadership to Danica's development in the Atlantic series. When her standing as a woman

>> CAREER TWILIGHT

Longtime family friend and team stalwart Jim Prescott congratulates Rahal as he steps out of his Reynard 98I Cosworth in his final race at the California Speedway on November 1, 1998, the 265th Champ Car start of his career. Prescott later ran Rahal's program for Danica Patrick in the Toyota Atlantic Series.

driver came under more intense pressure as the results in her initial 2003 season began to wane, Rahal stepped up for his young charge.

"Attention is a curse and a blessing for a young driver," he pointed out to the media. "When you succeed that spotlight is great because everyone will see your success, but when you meet with adversity, that spotlight can feel like it weighs a ton."

Having negotiated ups and downs in his own career, Rahal knew the value of having that kind of support.

"There has been a lot of attention focused on Danica as a driver and as a female in motorsports," he said, "but she has handled the attention like the pro she is."

For his part, Rahal was considering a change in the focus of his team and looking at what role Patrick's potential on ovals could play.

At the outset of the 1980s, CART appeared capable of the same growth experienced by NASCAR. But the CART format, where owners simultaneously ran the series and competed against one another, eventually fell prey to internal squabbles.

In 1996, Indianapolis Motor Speedway owner and president Tony George launched the Indy Racing League (IRL), a new open-wheel oval track race series. George made sure the new series kept the Indy 500 in its schedule by running separate rules for cars and

>> PODIUM PRESENCE

Now a full-time owner, Rahal joins the post-race celebration in victory lane with his two drivers at the Laguna Seca Raceway in 1999. Bryan Herta won the event in Shell colors and Max Papis came home third, the team's best result of its inaugural season without the founder in the cockpit.

engines under his own sanctioning body. Despite the fact that most of the big-name drivers and teams stayed on with the CART sanctioning body, whose brand name became Champ Car, the loss of the Indy 500 dealt a significant blow to the series.

Established drivers and team owners like A.J. Foyt won the Indy 500 during the late 1990s, but television ratings dwindled in the absence of the CART teams. The race began to find better traction with fans and viewers when the front-line teams of CART began returning, starting with the 2000 season. Toyota and Honda eventually switched to the IRL and returned to Indy as well. But the TV ratings for the 500 would not fully bounce back until Danica's appearance in the 2005 race.

For its part, the sanctioning body of CART dissolved in bankruptcy at the end of the 2003 season before re-emerging under new ownership. The series retained the name Champ Car and continued a schedule focused on road and street courses with standardized cars (Lola) and engines (Ford Cosworth) to keep costs in check.

Rahal had invested much of his career in the CART series as an owner, a driver, and an administrator, having served as the sanctioning body's interim president in 2000. Yet, by 2004 it became clear the split with the Indy Racing League eight years earlier and the subsequent withdrawal of CART from the Indy 500 had come with a high price. Rahal followed team owners Roger Penske, Chip Ganassi, and Michael Andretti in switching to the

continued on page 86

>> BRACK BREAKS THROUGH

Swede Kenny Brack brought Team Rahal four oval victories in 2001 and Italy's Max Papis captured two road course victories. Above: Brack and the team celebrate at the Chicago Motor Speedway in Cicero, Illinois, in July. Below Papis conquered the Champ Car entries at the Laguna Seca Raceway in October.

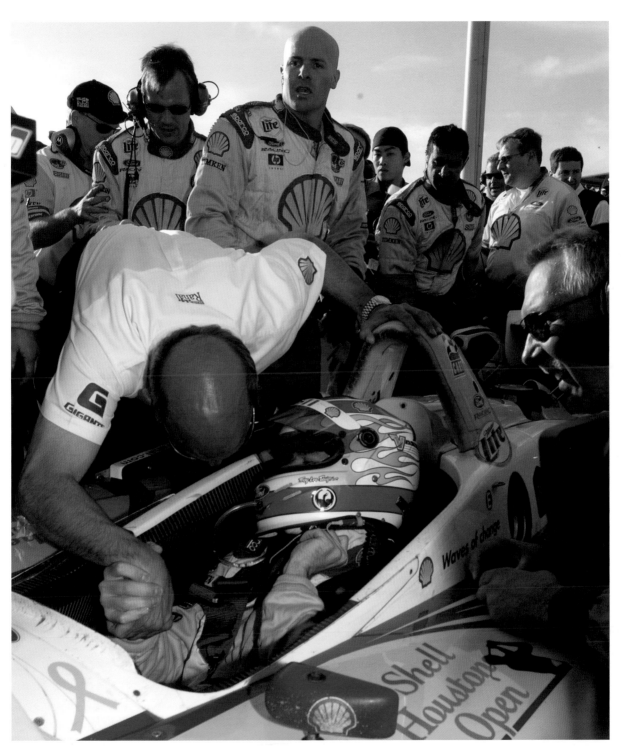

>> NEW DRIVER, SAME RESULTS

Rahal congratulates Jimmy Vasser after he won the California 500 by 0.600 seconds over Michael Andretti in 2002. The victory at the California Speedway was the fastest 500-mile race in history with an average speed of 197.995 miles per hour, breaking the old record by more than eight miles per hour.

>> TEAM WORKS

By 2003, Rahal had one Champ Car entry for Michel Jourdain, was running one car for Danica Patrick in the Atlantic series, and had launched his first full campaign in the Indy Racing League (IRL) with Kenny Brack. Below, Jourdain celebrates his first victory in Milwaukee, where Danica raced earlier in the day.

IRL full time along with the engine manufacturers. Once again he was banking on the Indy 500.

The renewed emphasis on Indy created new opportunities for the expansion of Rahal's partnership with Letterman. A native of Indianapolis, where he was considered a very funny guy by his classmates at Broad Ripple High School, Letterman remained a big fan of the Indy 500. When Letterman first met Rahal in 1986, the TV star had already been approached about buying into teams. Always a savvy salesman, Rahal kept his powder dry. He invited Letterman to the races, offering credentials and access instead of pitching him on buying into the team. The friendship continued to flourish.

continued on page 89

>> GETTING READY

Danica takes time off from her Toyota Atlantic Series campaign to visit with team owner Letterman and the rest of the Indy Racing League squad prior to the start of the 2004 Indianapolis 500. A short time later, Rahal confirmed she would move up to competition at Indy in 2005.

>> GRID GREETINGS

Letterman wishes Vitor Meira, a former South American F3 champion, good luck on the grid at the 2004 Indy 500, where he started seventh and finished sixth. In 2005, Meira stepped up, starting seventh and finishing second, two positions ahead of rookie teammate Danica Patrick.

>> GATHERING VICTORY

In the face of a storm brewing that would bring tornadoes to the Indianapolis area, Buddy Rice maintained his lead with the help of great pit stops and was in front when the 2004 race ended early after 180 laps. The team celebrated on the pit wall, but the storm forced Rice to celebrate in the garage.

Sutton/Swope

>> THE BOSS IS CALLING

An excerpt from The Late Show with David Letterman

David Letterman: What a tremendous day, what a wonderful experience (at the Indy 500). You could certainly feel that the crowd, like 400,000 people, all were just excited, and on the edge of their seats and standing the last 20 laps.

Danica Patrick: I've heard so much. You know I wish I could just hear the crowd for two seconds. Not for my ego or anything. (Laughter). But just to kind of, I don't know, be able to feel what the excitement was. Because so many people said it was just so loud you couldn't even hear the cars.

Letterman: Well, yeah, in addition to being loud, you kind of expect that. You got the sense that this group of people, all racing fans, had coalesced and their hearts were pulling for you. And the power of that is undeniable and just a wonderful experience. You have beautiful hair, by the way. (Laughter, applause)

Danica: I have to give it to the team backstage. They did my hair. You know the shampoo people aren't calling. This is a problem. I feel like I promote these products, you know, mortgage companies, TVs, car part things, windshield wipers. And, you know, the makeup and the hair people haven't been calling.

Letterman: We'll try to get you a shampoo deal. But don't feel bad. The shampoo people are not calling me, either. (Laughter)

>> BRINGING IT HOME

An elated Letterman, who grew up in Indianapolis, talks about winning the 2004 Indy 500 for the benefit of the TV audience. Little did he realize how much acclaim and excitement would be created the following year by a Rahal Letterman Racing driver who would finish fourth.

Ten years after they first met, Rahal called Letterman to see if he'd be interested in team ownership following the split with Hogan. Letterman accepted enthusiastically. Ironically, that was the same year CART split from the IRL and the Indy 500. Letterman remained a low-key minority owner in Team Rahal's CART operation and was an occasional race visitor, joking that he finally got a chance to meet famed actor Paul Newman, a partner at Newman/Haas Racing. Meanwhile, Letterman continued as a mainstay at the Indy 500, making an annual pilgrimage to the race.

Rahal's switch to IRL brought about the financial demands of building a three-car operation and presented a new opportunity with Letterman. Although the contracts are not made public, veteran racing observers considered the announcement of a name change to Rahal Letterman Racing in 2004 prior to the Indy 500 an indication that the Late Show host increased his role to co-ownership.

"David has been an integral part of the team's success over the past eight seasons and I can't think of a better way to honor his involvement than by renaming the team," Rahal said during the formal announcement.

Letterman remains a staunch supporter of the drivers and crew members at the races. He has not, Danica said, asked for any driving tips or a lift around the track on the sidepods of her Panoz-Honda.

But he is really observant, she said. "He's very into racing. He kind of sits there quietly and just observes what's going on, tries to lay low around us. I think that's really cool. He's definitely a guy who loves racing." ◇

CHAPTER FIVE

THE SPEEDWAY

"Make no mistake,

Danica is as feisty and as focused

and as tough a competitor

as I've ever been around in close to 30 years

of being part of this Indy 500."

—Jack Arute, ABC analyst, *New York Daily News*

The Indianapolis Motor Speedway's main grandstand runs forever and a day along Georgetown Road, parallel to the front straightaway. Once inside the confines of the track, a huge wall of stands and suites tower over the legendary track. The strip of bricks that cross the front straight are leftovers from nearly a century of legendary drivers testing their limits at the Indy 500.

When you walk along the track in the shadow of the towering grandstands, particularly in the quiet of the morning before the sounds of 10,000-rpm race engines and the smell of race fuel fill the air, the speedway has the feel of hallowed ground. You can almost sense the ghosts of greatness and the restless spirits of those who met tragic ends at the Indianapolis Motor Speedway.

The speedway's rich history is filled with tragedy, as the track's high speeds, flat corners, and high, hard outside walls are unforgiving to drivers who go astray. Virtually everybody working on pit road has known a driver who was seriously injured or killed at the legendary track.

Fear is only one of many psychological hurdles Indy presents to a new driver. Indy is unique in that the race spans nearly a month, including practice and qualifying. Each day has an ebb and flow that takes time and experience to master, which can be intimidating for a rookie.

The rectangular, slightly banked 2.5-mile circuit presents a unique racing challenge. Weather is a significant factor at the speedway, as the grandstands shelter and shadow the corners, causing conditions to change from lap to lap at times. The two long straightaways permit top speeds over 200 miles per hour, and the shadowed turns are often hard for drivers to see. The relatively short chute between Turn One and Turn Two demands careful line choice to set up for the next corner. The same is true in the chute between Turn Three and Turn Four. The backdrop of grandstands and the changes in exposure to sun, shadow, or wind make each corner a unique challenge despite their similar layouts.

With each passing year, crucial variables—such as chassis, tires, and the track surface—change along with the Indy Racing League (IRL) rule book that governs the event. This levels the playing field for rookies in qualifying. While the newcomers are struggling to learn the track, the veterans are sorting out new car setups. Once the new variables are taken into account, average speeds inevitably climb during practice as drivers adjust to the track and their setup.

Danica Patrick came to Indy well-equipped to deal with the challenges presented by the revered venue. She possessed a fine sense of balance and car control, an innate understanding of fast lines, and a battle-tested bravado. In addition, she had a strong outing in her previous race at Twin Ring Motegi in Japan. She had nearly won the pole versus old karting rival Sam Hornish Jr. and then jumped into the lead at the start of the race before finishing fourth.

>> HERO WORSHIP (PAGES 90-91)

A regular part of any driver's job is to meet the fans. Danica did her part at this year's Indianapolis 500 by giving autographs to many of her young female fans. *Michael Kim/LAT Photographic*

continued on page 95

>> HUNTING SPEED

For racers in the Indy 500, the month of May is spent practicing and qualifying. The long, grueling search for speed often takes a toll on drivers. Danica had the added pressure of dealing with a number of interview and appearance requests. *Brian Spurlock*

>> PATIENCE

Waiting in pit lane is part of the Indy experience, as the long days of practice and qualifying entail more

track time than any other race, plus intense engineering meetings to discuss car setup. *Brian Spurlock*

>> INDY ROOKIES

Danica attends the rookie drivers' meeting on Saturday before the 500, flanked by Champ Car champion Sebastien Bourdais on the right and Ryan Briscoe on the left. *Brian Spurlock*

Upon arriving at Indy, Patrick had already demonstrated she had the physical and psychological gearing necessary to step up from the 240-horsepower Atlantic cars with top speeds of 165 miles per hour to the 800-horsepower Indy cars. And she had demonstrated her ability to race with the best.

At Indy, it was more of the same. Danica immediately staked out her territory, starting with the car setup from teammates Buddy Rice and Vitor Meira, a third-year veteran from Brazil. Patrick was the first to pass rookie orientation on Day 1 and—after catching a draft from Tomas Enge—was the fastest among the newcomers in their full day of practice at 222.741 miles per hour.

But a driver can never be quite certain about practice speeds. The month-long extravaganza at Indy is made for head games as drivers struggle to find the fast setups. Are rival drivers faster because they got a tow in the draft down the straights, or did they do their quick lap solo? Who is half-lapping, working on one end of the speedway first for speed, then lifting off the throttle a bit at the other end without showing a full hot lap? Who had setups that will work in the race as well as qualifying?

Reducing aerodynamic downforce allows higher straightaway speeds but reduces traction in the corners. The increased speeds offer faster laps, but with less traction in the corners, spins become more likely. Qualifying well at Indy is a complicated formula that requires taking carefully calculated risks. As speeds push past 220 miles per hour, the demands to execute a perfect lap increase, as do the consequences of a mistake. If a driver loves gorging the brain and emotions on this heart-thumping process, then Indy really is close to

>> TEAM RAHAL

Team owner Bobby Rahal also kept a close eye on his other driver, the quiet, but effective Vitor Meira. *Brian Spurlock*

heaven, especially if your name is regularly close to the top of the daily speed charts.

Surprisingly, that's where Danica Patrick's name appeared, even after Days 1 and 2, which are reserved for rookie orientation. By Day 4, she was second to veteran Tony Kanaan, and by Day 5, she led the charts

at 227.633 miles per hour before dropping back to third on "Fast Friday" behind Tomas Scheckter and Kanaan. Two significant factors made a difference for Patrick. First, some patches of uneven pavement forced the speedway to diamond-grind the entire surface, making its texture noticeably different from the previous year. Tire construction and compounds from Firestone had also changed to accommodate the new surface, giving all the veterans significantly different variables.

>> WALKING THE LANE

The crowd is cleared out as Danica makes her way to the starting grid.

>> INDY ROOKIES

The finishes of all of the rookie of the year drivers in the Indy Racing League (1996–present) are shown, along with some other significant Indy rookies.

ROOKIE YEAR	DRIVER	INDY 500 STARTING POSITION	SPEED	INDY 500 FINISHING POSITION	LAPS COMPLETED (REASON OUT)	ROOKIE OF THE YEAR	INDY 500 WINS
2000	Juan Pablo Montoya	2	223.372 mph	1	200 laps	Juan Pablo Montoya	1
2001	Helio Castroneves	11	224.142 mph	1	200 laps	Helio Castroneves	2
1928	Louis Meyer	13	111.352 mph	1	200 laps	No rookie award	3
1926	Frank Lockhart	20	95.783 mph	1	160 laps (rain)	No rookie award	1
1994	Jacques Villeneuve	4	160.749 mph	2	200 laps	Jacques Villeneuve	1
1965	Mario Andretti	4	158.849 mph	3	200 laps	Mario Andretti	1
1997	Jeff Ward	7	214.517 mph	3	200 laps	Jeff Ward	0
1998	Steve Knapp	23	216.440 mph	3	200 laps	Steve Knapp	0
2005	Danica Patrick	4	227.004 mph	4	200 laps	Danica Patrick	0
1927	Wilbur Shaw	19	104.465 mph	4	200 laps	No rookie award	3
2002	Alex Barron	26	228.580 mph	4	200 laps	Alex Barron (co)	0
2003	Tora Takagi	7	229.358 mph	5	200 laps	Tora Takagi	0
1952	Art Cross	20	134.288 mph	5	200 laps	Art Cross	0
1999	Robby McGehee	27	220.139 mph	5	199 laps	Robby McGehee	0
1911	Ralph De Palma	2	NA	6	200 laps	No rookie award	1
1965	Al Unser	32	154.440 mph	9	196 laps	Mario Andretti	4
1919	Gaston Chevrolet	16	100.400 mph	10	200 laps	No rookie award	1
1982	Bobby Rahal	17	194.770 mph	11	174 laps (engine)	Jim Hickman	1
1992	Lyn St. James	27	220.150 mph	11	193 laps	Lyn St. James	0
1958	A.J. Foyt	12	143.130 mph	16	148 laps (spun and hit wall)	George Amick	4
1996	Tony Stewart	1	233.100 mph	24	82 laps (engine)	Tony Stewart	0
2002	Tomas Scheckter	10	229.058 mph	26	172 laps (accident)	Tomas Scheckter (co)	0
1951	Bill Vukovich	20	133.725 mph	29	29 laps (oil tank)	No rookie award	2
1963	Johnny Rutherford	26	148.063 mph	29	143 laps (transmission)	Jim Clark	3
1977	Janet Guthrie	26	188.403 mph	29	27 laps (timing gear)	Jerry Sneva	0
2004	Mark Taylor	14	219.282 mph	30	62 laps (accident)	Mark Taylor	0
2000	Sarah Fisher	19	220.237 mph	31	71 laps (accident)	Juan Pablo Montoya	0
1963	Bobby Unser	16	149.421 mph	33	2 laps (spun and hit wall)	Jim Clark	3
1933	Mauri Rose	42	117.649 mph	35	48 laps (timing gear)	No rookie award	2

An insider at Rahal Letterman Racing suggested an irregular grinding of the surface at Turn Two had surprised defending champion Buddy Rice, who suffered a snap spin and backed into the wall on Day 4, leaving him with a concussion and severely strained ligaments in his neck.

The 2005 update kit on the Panoz chassis could have been another factor in Rice's crash. The revised underside of the 2005 chassis created too much downforce. The setup teams used to compensate occasionally pinned the nose of the car. Whatever the cause, Rice was out for the 500.

continued on page 100

The traditional unleashing of the ballons signals the start of the 89th running of the Indianapolis 500 on May 29, 2005. After 500 miles of some of the most high-speed racing in the world, someone in the field will capture the coveted Borg-Warner Trophy. *Brian Spurlock*

>> STARTING LINEUP

The diminutive Danica takes her place with the other 32 drivers on the fabled yard of bricks at the start-finish line of the Indianapolis Motor Speedway, just prior to the start of the race.

The Rahal team would run only cars for Meira, who had worked with Patrick's engineer Ray Leto the year before, and Patrick in the first week of qualifying. When rain pelted the speedway on the first day of qualifying, it gave Patrick more time to think about trying to win the pole prize that eluded her at Motegi by 31 thousandths of a second. A pole at Indy would definitely confirm, yet again, she was for real.

"You don't want to do anything that makes you doubt the car," she said in a heavily attended media conference on the rainy Saturday. "You have to have the most confidence in the world in your car and that you're going to keep your foot down," she continued, adding that it was important to avoid the same problem Rice had suffered by pinning the front end. "If the car is too positive in the front, you're going to slip at the front end and hit the wall trying to keep your foot in it. So I think the first lap has to be a confidence builder and knowing where

the car is going to be. The second lap you've got to push it and go after it."

On Sunday morning, all had drastically changed, due to suddenly chilly weather as well as a "green" track (rain had washed off all the rubber put down in practice). Drivers were turned loose for one final practice session prior to qualifying, and Patrick again turned in a stunner. On a track open to every driver under the same conditions, Danica scorched the time sheets, albeit with the help of the draft. Her lap of 229.422 miles per hour was the fastest of the month, in part due to cooler ambient temperatures that generated more Honda horsepower and a spot-on qualifying setup from her engineer Leto. Gasoline Alley, the suites, pit road, and the grandstands buzzed with excitement; Danica Patrick could become the first woman to win the Indy 500 pole.

When Patrick rolled out of the pits shortly after noon on May 15, 2005, the object was to run four laps on the

>> FULL HOUSE

The Indy 500 has always drawn big crowds, but Danica helped sell some tickets in 2005. She also significantly raised TV viewership and public awareness about the race that is scheduled for Memorial Day weekend. *Brian Spurlock*

Rahal Letterman driver Vitor Meira is strapped in and ready to challenge the Indy 500.

ragged edge of control in a car trimmed for minimal downforce. Inevitably, the midday conditions on Sunday were different than those in the morning. A higher air temperature meant tire temperatures would change and downforce, which changes with the density of the air, would be lower. After three warm-up laps to get heat in her tires, Danica shot into Turn One at full throttle on faith and guts in a car tuned to her engineer's best estimate for the track conditions.

After her driving line took the left front wheel beneath the white line marking the apron, Patrick's momentous slide began. As the rear end stepped out, she used years of road racing experience and uncanny

>> HELPING HAND
Rahal and Danica's fiancé Paul Hospenthal (he and Danica plan to wed in November 2005) spend time preparing the rookie during the final moments before the start of the Indy 500.

>> RACE FACE

Danica moments before the start of the biggest race of her career to date.

rookie skills on a high-speed oval to save her car. The slip slowed her first lap to a relatively slow 224 miles per hour. Danica stayed poised and recorded three successive laps of 227 miles per hour, the last one the fastest any driver turned in during qualifying that day—227.860 miles per hour. The team had nailed the setup and Patrick nearly wrung the most from it. But the slip through Turn One cost her the pole.

"The wind changed, the temperatures changed, and that changed the downforce on the car," she said after qualifying. "It's frustrating. I want to be on pole."

Moments later, highly touted rookie Ryan Briscoe spun and crashed in Turn One, a further testament to the difficulty of this corner where the entry is partially blocked from the driver's view by the south end of the pit wall.

Two hours later, Patrick remained highly focused while sequestered in the team's garage in Gasoline Alley, her voracious appetite to prove herself still in high gear while awaiting the outcome of teammate Meira's qualifying run. It ended just a shade below her average speed for four circuits. After telling her engineer Leto that she wanted to try again, Danica asked: "Where are the bosses?"

Rahal and team manager Scott Roembke returned from the pit road to huddle with their driver and her engineer. But after four more laps of practice with a different setup (including more fuel to change the balance), Patrick's speed did not pick up. With one driver already on the sideline and Kenny Brack due to qualify the next weekend as a substitute for Rice, the team had plenty of work to keep busy. Instead of risking a crash, the team elected to stand on its time for the No. 16 Panoz-Honda despite new rules that allowed three attempts per day.

As things turned out, the decision to stand on Danica's time was a sound one that landed her a starting position

>> FINALLY . . .

All the planning, practice, media conferences, sponsor appearances, autograph sessions, and testing are done. As the cars roll off for the start, it's just Danica, her car and team, against 32 other drivers.

of fourth on the grid for the Indy 500. It was the highest starting position for any woman in the history of the 500, proof of a changing order. Under the long shadow of grandstands that have witnessed some of the greatest entrances in the history of motorsports, Danica Patrick met the track's challenges with grace, skill, and heart. The fans took note, and the media responded with a frenzy that included tracking Danica's every move off the track in the Daily Trackside Report. The ghosts of Indy may have been somewhat dismayed by the frenzy, but they would have approved of Patrick's gutsy performance on the track.

Danica, however, was not satisfied. She is a racer, and racers never settle for second place.

RACE DAY

Danica got her chance to run up front in the closing laps of the Indy 500. When she slid past Dan Wheldon to take the lead, the mammoth crowd roared its approval. Happy to see Danica Patrick as the new race leader with 11 laps to go, the throng waved arms and caps at every turn of the speedway, hurrying car No. 16 toward the finish line.

Patrick had run the fastest lap in the month of May driving for Rahal Letterman Racing, the defending champions. She had led the speed charts in the final practice session. Starting on the inside of Row 2, she had become the first woman to lead the Indy 500 long before the halfway mark. With 27 laps to go, she had ridden in first place behind the safety car awaiting a restart.

>> THE PACE LAP

Patrick started the race in the fourth position, slotted in between pole sitter Tony Kanaan (foreground) and teammate Vitor Meira. *Brian Spurlock*

The battle between Patrick and Dan Wheldon for the lead of the 2005 Indianapolis 500 had the world wondering if this would be the historic year in which a woman would win the Borg-Warner Trophy. *Sutton/Swope*

Yet there was an element of surprise in the delight over a possible Patrick victory. People pointed, turned to one another, shaking their heads in disbelief. The prospect of a 5-foot 2-inch, 100-pound woman winning the toughest, most dangerous speed contest since the dawn of the automobile was hard to grasp.

What would it mean if the same race won four times by ornery, flinty Texan A. J. Foyt suddenly had this little brunette hugging the silver trophy that was almost as big as her? The mere possibility of this outcome captured the imagination of America's sports fans and brought the 350,000-plus fans in attendance to their feet.

After leading three laps early on, Danica stalled during her third pit stop, surely the end of her victory hopes as leaders Sam Hornish Jr., Tony Kanaan, Dario Franchitti, and Danica's teammate Vitor Meira whipped around at an average breathtaking pace of 225 miles per hour.

Brent Musburger, the veteran broadcaster hosting the ABC telecast, perhaps spoke for many when he called Danica the "darling" of the event. He intoned how wonderful it would be if she managed to finish in the top 10.

The TV crew may have written Patrick off as a top contender, but her team knew this driver had a habit of ratcheting her way back through the field. Much like Foyt once did, Danica punched into an extra gear when the going got tough. After the pit road mistake dropped her to 16th position, she let loose some frustration in an outburst of unprintable words and then channeled her fury into getting back in the race.

Always a quick study, she started learning about how to set people up for a pass. She steadily leap-frogged lapped traffic and those competing for position, moving up the scoreboard as the laps wound down. Two cautions

>> PACKED PITS

Almost all the competitors made a pit stop under an early caution. Rahal Letterman driver Kenny Brack was one of the first back out, but 30 other cars are about to join him. *Sutton/Swope*

>> ROOKIE MISTAKE

Teammate Kenny Brack leaves the pits in front of Danica. A pit miscue early in the race temporarily dropped Patrick to the mid-field.

>> BACK IN FRONT

For the second time in the race, Danica leads the Indy 500. Coming into Turn One, Dan Wheldon—
along with the rest of the field—is close behind. *Michael Kim/LAT Photographic*

for crashes involving veterans who cut it too close in traffic—the 2003 IRL champion Scott Dixon and two-time champ Hornish Jr.—helped Patrick's progress by bunching the field under yellow flags prior to restarts. She whipped underneath Kosuke Matsuura at the apex of Turn Four with such astounding quickness that her rear tire had clipped his left front with a puff of smoke before the Japanese driver could even consider changing his line.

This was magical stuff for a newcomer to high-speed ovals and 800-horsepower cars on a day when two veterans had already crashed. Within 60 laps of her

stall, Danica had regained eighth place. Then another setback occurred shortly after the cleanup was completed for Hornish Jr.'s accident. With 45 laps remaining, another rookie mistake cost Patrick time.

As the leaders bunched behind the safety car approaching Turn Four in anticipation of the green flag, Patrick's excessive speed forced her to the high line to avoid seventh-placed Scott Sharp. On cold tires and now outside the groove in the spent rubber grit thrown off by tires, Patrick's car spun sideways.

The driver behind her, fellow rookie Tomas Enge, tried to avoid the spin but hit No. 16 in the nose, knocking off

>> A SOLID OUTING

Vitor Meira quietly went about his business on race day. He didn't make any headlines, but he did finish second in the 2005 Indy 500.

>> THE LUCK OF THE DRAW

Team Rahal driver and former Indy 500 winner Kenny Brack in the pits. Brack's day ended on lap 92, when he left the race with a mechanical problem and finished 26th.

the left front wing. As Patrick's car pin-wheeled an entire loop the opposite direction, other cars took evasive action at roughly 100 miles per hour.

As the saying goes in racing, sometimes it's better to be lucky than good. Where Enge and teammate Tomas Sheckter each wrecked their Dallara chassis in the free-for-all, Patrick's Panoz ended up pointed toward the

entrance to pit road, where she trundled in aboard her damaged car. With the poise of a veteran, she had kept the engine running.

Her team, also poised in the pits, replaced the nose cone as Danica shouted, "Lead lap! Lead lap!" over the radio. Led by engineer Leto, the Rahal Letterman team had two tasks: first, to be sure the No. 16 was properly

>> APPLAUSE IN THE PITS

Danica's crew celebrates a solid performance at the 2005 Indy 500. She finished a competitive fourth in her rookie appearance at Indy.

>> RAHAL AND PATRICK

Team leader Bobby Rahal was the first to greet Danica in pit lane after her remarkable rookie Indy
500 performance.

repaired and sent back out while still on the lead lap; and second, to plot strategy for the final 46 laps of the race.

The Rahal team elected to play a traditional high-low poker bet familiar to those who follow Indy car racing. Their "high card" would be veteran Meira, designated to continue his race at the front versus Andretti Green's Dan Wheldon, Tony Kanaan, and Dario Franchitti. Patrick, meanwhile, would run the "low card," or a fuel strategy.

>> CONGRATS, KID

As the dust settled immediately after the race, Danica gives her father, T. J., a big hug in the pit lane.

Like the Rahal team, Andretti Green was playing the high-low gambit, running Wheldon, Kanaan, and Franchitti as its high card racers, with a full load of fuel and the team's fourth car driven by Bryan Herta on a fuel strategy. Penske Racing, meanwhile, was down to one entry after Sam Hornish Jr. crashed. The team decided two-time Indy 500 winner Helio Castroneves did not have the pace to win on speed and ran its lone remaining entry on a fuel-saving strategy.

The cars of Patrick, Herta, and Castroneves (the low-card, or fuel-saving players) ducked back into the pits under the last lap of the caution period to top off fuel with just over 40 laps remaining. Any of the cars on the fuel strategy had a chance to win the race. But Patrick, Herta, and Castroneves would have to cut back on the fuel mixture settings in their cockpits to make it to the finish and therefore run relatively slower. On the other hand, with some luck, yellow flag laps would save fuel and enable them to possibly run on full fuel settings in the closing laps.

The "high card" leaders (Wheldon, Kanaan, Meira, and Franchitti) could afford to run the maximum fuel settings for their engines, and hence run a faster pace under more power. They would consume more fuel this way and make one additional pit stop. Restarting in the back, Patrick's job had suddenly changed. She needed to conserve fuel, a difficult art, and stay ahead of the other two competitors running the same strategy—all while running in the turbulent air at the back of the field, loaded with ill-handling backmarkers.

"It sucks back there," Patrick later said. Via her radio, she told her crew, "I'm sorry."

As the laps wound down, the minor miracle anticipated by Rahal Letterman's pit strategists came to pass. When the "high card" leaders Wheldon, Meira, Franchitti, and Kanaan pitted for a final load of fuel at lap 171 of 200, Patrick rolled into the lead behind the safety car on the front straight. The "high card" leaders, meanwhile, rejoined the tail end of the line behind the safety car with plenty of fuel to run flat out to the finish.

>> **DAIRY DAN**

At the end of the day, it was Dan Wheldon, not Danica Patrick, that got to drink the milk and go into the record books as the winner of the 89th running of the Indianapolis 500. *Sutton/Swope*

Like a wave, the fans rose to their feet as the red and blue car with the gold No. 16 rolled past behind the pace car in first place. They shouted, whooped, and pointed, not just tipping their caps but waving them in salute.

Patrick hustled away on the restart with 27 laps to go, one lapped car between her and Herta's Dallara-Honda. She maintained the lead and the gap for 14 laps. But was she using too much fuel to stay ahead? Was Herta hanging back in the draft on a leaner fuel mixture setting, saving his methanol for a flat-out finish?

Suddenly, Wheldon passed Patrick for the lead under maximum Honda power on full fuel settings, just as another yellow came out when Matsuura hit the wall in Turn Three.

With the pack bunched up under caution, it would be a fight to the finish after the restart. In second place, Danica needed "the restart of the century" when the green flag flew again, her engineer Ray Leto told her over the radio. At the green with 11 laps to go, the rookie dropped back in traffic on the front straight, then expertly picked up the draft and ducked inside Wheldon at Turn One for the lead!

The cement stands rocked as the crowd roared its approval in the biggest response ever heard at the speedway.

"That was a lot louder than the cheer I got when I passed Kevin Cogan at Turn One," Rahal said of his emotional and popular victory for Jim Trueman's team.

Alas, Patrick needed still more yellow flag laps to save fuel. In the meantime, she had to cut back on the fuel mixture and power once again. Wheldon retook the lead four tense green flag laps later under full fuel settings and full throttle. Meira and Herta came past next on richer fuel settings, Herta having indeed saved fuel in the draft. In a break for Patrick, the crash of rookie Sebastien Bourdais brought out one final yellow with two laps to go, ensuring she would be able to roll to the finish without running out of fuel. Team Rahal had reason to celebrate—Meira had placed second, Patrick fourth, both behind a strong performance by Wheldon.

In the post-race media conference, Danica congratulated second-placed Meira for "kicking butt" and lamented her own situation, a gamble at best.

"It was frustrating to be leading the race with so few laps to go and not be able to just hang out up front and win the thing," she said.

As to whether she realized the historical importance of what she had accomplished that day—being the first woman to lead a lap at the Indy 500 and being the top woman finisher—Danica further demonstrated her focus on racing, rather than the hype surrounding her performance.

"I don't know," she said. "I'm just racing. It sounds so goober stupid, but I just don't think about it."

Of course, there was the obligatory question about "making a hell of a point for the females" from one of the reporters, which Danica quickly responded to.

"Are you kidding me?" she replied. "I made a hell of a point for anybody." ◇

CHAPTER SIX

THE ROOKIE SEASON

"If I'm doing something,

it's because I feel I can beat everyone;

I feel like I can win."

— Danica Patrick, *Sports Illustrated*

>>> >>> >>> >>> >>> >>> >>> >>> >>> >>>

With her strong performance at the 2005 Indy 500, Danica Patrick instantly became one of America's new sports heroes. She was everywhere—magazine covers and countless sports and talk TV shows. Because her appeal reached across generations—drawing admiration from young women who didn't know anything about racing as well as veteran fans—Danica could do everything from ESPN *SportsCenter* to chatting with Letterman.

The glare of the limelight fell midway in her rookie season, but Patrick withstood the media pressure with such confidence that one aging sportswriter compared her entrance to that of Arnold Palmer. At times, the media turned into something akin to Arnie's Army, following her every move at a racetrack to see what might happen next, just like the crowds following the golfer's early days at the Masters. Veteran columnist David Kindred sent her a valentine through the *Sporting News,* writing, "I don't care if she wears a parka. I love that woman." Patrick's ability to shake up what *Sports Illustrated* dubbed the "celebrity industrial complex" made her more than a race car driver—she became a one-woman cultural revolution.

"It takes a lot more than just driving a fast car," Patrick said when asked about her ease in the spotlight. "You have to present yourself well. You have to represent your sponsors well. I think I've always known that. You have to have something inside of you. Some people are shy and probably won't ever get there. You have to be comfortable and confident. The more you do it, the better you become."

Many people credited this newcomer with reviving the fortune of the Indy Racing League, launched by

Indianapolis Motor Speedway owner and president Tony George as a rival to Champ Car in 1996.

"Danica has brought more fans to the track and is a big part of our increased TV ratings," Indy 500 winner and IRL regular Dan Wheldon told motorsport.com. "I think she's doing an absolutely excellent job."

Ratings for the Indy 500 alone soared 60 percent, recording a 6.5 Nielsen rating, the best since the split with Champ Car nine years earlier.

"The last few years, I had been thinking [that] if I can get into the IRL, I just know I can help and make a difference," Danica said. "I thought if our team can just do well on the track, great things can happen. It probably is even bigger than what I thought it was going to be, or faster . . . But it all happened so fast. I think you have to have big dreams."

A rare young athlete had arrived, but in the rush to create a new celebrity the general media overlooked the problems rookie drivers face. Even a race car driver whose success had moved her from the sports pages to the front page of major newspapers could not escape the development curve imposed by motor racing.

No great drivers in the twentieth century had popped up without prior experience and won major league events (unless you count Cole Trickle from the Tom Cruise movie *Days of Thunder*). Those like Earnhardt, Andretti, and Foyt all had to deal with radical changes in equipment and the playing fields as they moved up to becoming legends. And none of the experienced

>> PIKES PEAK (PAGES 114-115)
Danica on the mike at Pikes Peak Raceway in August 2005. In the race, she qualified fifth and finished eighth. *Sutton/Swope*

>> THE 500

After Danica was fast all month at Indy and led the race, the media coverage propelled her to instant celebrity. Although she had been dealing with the media and sponsors for a long time, Danica attracted a whole new level of attention post-Indy. *Michael Kim/LAT Photographic*

competitors they went up against ever slowed down and waited for the newcomer to catch up.

"It's a huge learning curve," Buddy Lazier, the winner of the 1996 Indy 500, told *The New York Times*. A former Indy Racing League champion, Lazier predicted "bigger and better things" from Patrick after she had oriented herself to the series.

But those bigger and better things had to come amid a flurry of interview requests and endorsement opportunities. Danica had more on her mind than just learning how to handle a new car, team, and road courses.

She also had to deal with a few drivers who still thought she didn't belong. Robby Gordon, an on-again, off-again participant in the Indy 500 and a NASCAR regular, said he wouldn't want to race Danica because she had an unfair weight advantage. Weighing in at 100 pounds, she was considerably lighter than most other drivers.

"The lighter the car, the faster the speed," Gordon said. "Do the math."

Fifty to seventy fewer pounds in the cockpit of a 1,550-pound IRL car could have a tick of an influence in qualifying. Yet nobody had ever complained in the

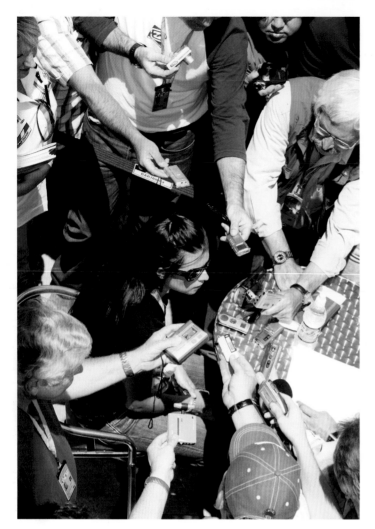

>> **MANICA**

Just a few weeks after the Indy 500, Danica is back at Indy for the U.S. Grand Prix Formula 1 race. She wasn't driving, but she was still besieged by fans and the international press. *Sutton Images*

previous two seasons about Vitor Meira, Patrick's team-mate, who weighed 130 pounds, significantly less than some of the taller, heavier IRL drivers.

"They don't lower the rims for shorter players in the NBA," said Danica, defending her turf.

The IRL contemplated a change in the rules to accommodate the weight disparity between drivers, as is done in NASCAR and Formula 1. But the message behind Gordon's comments was clear: Danica posed enough of a threat that any advantage might make her difficult to beat.

Patrick responded to the controversy by winning poles at Kansas City, Kentucky, and Chicago, 1.5-mile banked tracks where the Panoz chassis qualified comparably to the Dallaras. She also started third on the banked tracks in Texas and on the outside front row in Nashville. Patrick's Honda had a 20-horsepower advantage over those running Toyota engines while Chevy's engines ranked in between.

One week after the Indy 500, the race in Ft. Worth, Texas, turned into a media circus. Hordes of print journalists and TV cameras followed every move by America's hottest race car driver, including a pre-race jaunt to the port-a-john. The race, where she finished 13th after a rough night's education in the dirty air of mid-pack traffic, marked the beginning of the "Danica Win Watch."

This, too, put her on the defensive, especially when distant finishes followed front row starts.

"I'm very early in my career," Patrick said.

"I've done so little oval racing, and there's just so many things that are new to me. People who are close to racing and know what is going on in the sport understand where I'm at in the learning curve. They have a good grasp of what's going on each and every weekend and they understand that this is a process that takes time. Nobody wants me to win more than I want to win for myself. With media expectations or without expectations, I will give the same effort and try just as hard for that win."

In the nine races after Indy, Patrick finished on the lead lap just three times, her best finish being seventh at Nashville.

"I'm finding that all the tracks are a little bit different," she said. "Some of the time the corners are banked more than others. Other times they're more of a one-groove track than a two-groove, or two and three. They all have their little differences, bumps and whatnot."

The Panoz chassis run by Danica's team was also a factor. During that same stretch, only one driver—Scott Sharp—scored a victory in a Panoz chassis.

>> TAKING IT TO THE STREETS

Prior to the Indy 500, Danica had started her season not unlike any other rookie with a new team. Here, Danica is in the first IRL street race in St. Petersburg, Florida, the third race of the 2005 season. *Sutton/Swope*

Patrick said some of her days at the track would be better than others.

"They always say on an oval when you're running good, it's a lot of fun, and when you're not, it's just a long day," she said. "And that's true. I did the best I could, especially at Michigan, to improve the car."

She was learning how to adjust the car's handling while on the track, using controls in the cockpit to make anti-roll bar adjustments for the front and rear suspensions at speeds well in excess of 200 miles per hour.

"I was definitely trying to make it handle and be drivable," she said. "It was really hard."

Although Patrick resides in Phoenix, she grew up in the Chicago area. After a four-month whirlwind of media engagements, sponsor events, and the business of signing endorsements, the IRL race at the 1.5-mile Chicagoland Speedway was a bit of a homecoming for Danica. Unlike most of the superspeedway ovals where she raced as a rookie, a Honda-sponsored test on the 1.5-mile Chicagoland Speedway enabled Patrick to turn laps before the typical two-day IRL race weekend began.

By the season's 15th of 17 events, Patrick had developed more confidence in her ability to sort a car while setting up for qualifying and the race.

>> BIG IN JAPAN

In her fourth start, Patrick had her best race of the year at the fantastic oval at Twin Ring Motegi in Japan. She qualified second and finished fourth behind teammate Buddy Rice. Indy was next on the schedule. *Sutton/Swope*

>> FAN FAVORITE

After the 2005 Indy 500, the IRL moved to Texas. Danica's wide exposure in the press, including a *Sports Illustrated* cover (left), made her more popular than ever with the fans. *Michael L. Levitt/LAT Photographic*

>> MISHAP PAYDAY

After a Danica rookie mistake took out Tomas Enge at Indy, the two auctioned off this autographed piece of front wing from the incident two weeks later at Texas. It raised $42,650 for charity. *Dave Vaughn/ LAT Photographic*

"That's something that I probably have always been able to do," she said. "That's what makes us drivers. One of the things that develops is your trust, for me anyway. I've had to develop the trust that I'm right. If the team made a big change on the car, I'll come back into the pits and they'll say, 'What did that do?' If I don't feel anything, I've got to say, 'I don't feel anything'."

Ultimately, there are limits when teams miss on the chassis setups relative to the other drivers and teams.

"If the car can't do it, the car can't do it," said Patrick. "You can't force it."

That's a familiar plight to any race car driver, but Patrick went through the process with tremendous expectation following the Indy 500.

As much as any other event outside of Indy, the Chicago race demonstrated her ability to steadily improve her lap times before going all-out for the pole. After year-long complaints that she immediately dropped back at the start of races—a favorite comment in chat rooms—Patrick led the first lap at Chicago by aggressively exploiting the inside line.

The banked oval track requires driver's to run in tightly-packed clusters of cars at 210 miles per hour. Racing in such close quarters at high speeds requires a balance of aggressiveness, patience, and discipline that is typically difficult for rookie drivers to balance.

Patrick demonstrated her mastery of the banked ovals at Chicago. She stuck with the low line in the early going at Chicago until Byran Herta ran three-wide at the exit of Turn Four, forcing her onto the apron. For the first time, Patrick made a savvy move in the higher second groove on the outside, making the pass stick and taking back fifth place from Herta.

The moves by her fellow contenders for rookie of the year, Australia's Ryan Briscoe and the Czech Republic's Tomas Enge, told a different tale in Chicago. Briscoe's

>> THE T-SHIRT SAYS IT ALL

When Patrick's teammate Buddy Rice wore a T-shirt that read "Danica's Teammate," Vitor Meira came up with his own take on the matter. *Phillip Abbott/LAT Photographic*

>> THE PRESS

As the Indy Racing League moves further into the summer, the interest in Danica remains high. Here she talks to the press at Richmond International Raceway on June, 25, 2005. *Sutton Images*

ill-advised dash into Turn Three resulted in a horrifying crash that sent the Formula 1 test driver for Toyota into the hospital with a concussion, two broken clavicles, and a collapsed lung. Enge, the de facto Formula 3000 champion in Formula 1's understudy series in 2002, hit the wall midway in the race, damaging his suspension.

Before the race, Helio Castroneves had praised Patrick's pilgrim's progress when it came to learning the draft at the intermediate, 1.5-mile banked tracks where cars constantly joust for position in laps lasting a mere 25 seconds.

"A lot of young guys just go for it," he said in praise of Patrick's more conservative method.

Certainly Briscoe, driving for the front-line Target Chip Ganassi Racing team, and Enge, driving for Panther

>> POLE POSITION

At Kansas in July, Danica wins her first pole position in the IRL. *Sutton Images*

>> FAST FEET

Danica trades a pair of shoes with six-time Olympic champion Jackie Joyner-Kersee at Pikes Peak in August 2005. *Michael L. Levitt/LAT Photographic*

>> THE STREETS OF SAN FRAN

Patrick drives through the streets of San Francisco in her Rahal Letterman Racing Panoz-Honda to promote the upcoming race at Infineon Raceway. *Sutton Images*

>> OUT FOR THE DAY

Danica is consoled by fellow driver Helio Castroneves after a racing incident with Ryan Briscoe left them both wrecked at Infineon Raceway, the road course in Sonoma, California. *Lesley Ann Miller/LAT Photographic*

Racing's renown squad, had been going for it much of the season. Briscoe's exit at Chicago was his seventh accident, not including practice mishaps. Enge's retirement comprised his third accident of the season, not including Patrick's spin at Indy or a crash attributed to suspension failure at Nashville. The latter crash forced Enge to miss two races with a back injury.

With the help of pit strategy and by skipping a tire change on her last stop, Patrick finished sixth at Chicago, receiving a form of praise from Tony Kanaan afterward.

"Danica Patrick is an idiot," fumed the Andretti Green driver and defending series champion after he failed to get past Patrick on the low line late in the race.

At last, she was being treated like any other competitor!

Patrick's first season in the IRL was a strong one, but it was not without the usual rookie mistakes and accidents. At the Homestead, Florida, opener in March, she failed to slow for a caution, clipped another car, and careened into the wall heavily. A concussion cost her 30 minutes of memory.

A second self-induced accident occurred at Milwaukee in July, where her Panoz spun into the wall after she had advanced back through the field to sixth place despite a loose-handling chassis.

In August, at the series' first road circuit race in history on the 12-turn Infineon Raceway circuit in Sonoma, California, pole starter Briscoe dived to the inside of Patrick's Panoz at Turn Seven in a moment of brain fade. Briscoe's Panoz slid into the dirt under braking before he crashed into Patrick, who in turn hit Castroneves. Briscoe later apologized to both for knocking them out of the race.

Up until that three-car incident at Infineon, pit strategy clearly failed to help Patrick navigate one of America's most challenging road courses. The heavy aerodynamic downforce used by the IRL race cars on road courses and resulting demands on upper torso strength reversed any size advantage Patrick had on ovals.

IRL race cars use sculpted aerodynamics to generate heavy downforce. The car's bodywork forms an airfoil, like an airplane wing, except the car's aerodynamics press down while an airplane's press up to provide lift. IRL cars set up for road course racing create thousands of pounds of downforce. This gives the tires more traction and allows the car to go through the corners at incredible speeds. That much downforce also makes the steering wheel hard to turn.

On an oval course, where the steering adjustments are incremental and downforce is typically run at lighter

>> CHI-TOWN HUSTLE

In only her 14h IRL start, at Chicagoland Speedway, Danica was on the pole for the third time. Here she leads at the start with Rahal Letterman teammate Buddy Rice on the outside of the front row.
Sutton/Swope

settings, this is not a significant factor for a small driver like Danica. The tight, twisting turns of a road course, on the other hand, require the driver to wrestle the heavy-steering cars through the corners.. This was a challenge for Patrick, whose size advantage on the ovals was neutralized at Infineon.

"On a road course, you need to be able to push and pull, grab the wheel hard," she said. "There's long and short corners. You need to be able to have the endurance, but you need to be able to have the sheer strength to turn the wheel sometimes."

By time she left the second road circuit on the schedule at Watkins Glen in September, where she finished 16th,

Patrick had clinched the IRL rookie-of-the-year title, matching the same honor from the Indy 500.

Throughout her struggle to score the first victory, Patrick remained philosophical.

"As long as I'm learning and changed something in the past that I'd done wrong maybe, or as a team we've done wrong, and improved on it, that's a victory," said Patrick. "I feel as long as we keep doing that, we're moving in the right direction. It's just a matter of time before I'm running in the front more consistently, and the inevitable will happen. I'll be in a position to win my first race."

Certainly, nobody would be counting Danica Patrick out in her second appearance at the Indy 500 in 2006. ◇

RACE RESULTS

NDY RACING LEAGUE—2005 >> Team: Rahal Letterman Racing >> Car: Panoz 2004-Honda H15R

TRACK	LOCATION	START	FINISH	LAPS COMPLETED	
Homestead-Miami Speedway	Homestead, Fla.	9	15	158/200	(accident)
Phoenix International Raceway	Phoenix, Ariz.	18	15	194/200	
St. Petersburg, Fla.	Street circuit	15	12	95/100	
Twin Ring Motegi	Japan	2	4	200/200	
Indianapolis Motor Speedway	Indianapolis, Ind.	4	4	200/200	
Texas Motor Speedway	Ft. Worth, Texas	3	13	200/200	
Richmond International Raceway	Richmond, Va.	21	10	247/250	
Kansas Speedway	Kansas City, Kan.	1	9	200/200	
Nashville Superspeedway	Nashville, Tenn.	2	7	200/200	
The Milwaukee Mile	Milwaukee, Wisc.	6	19	125/225	(accident)
Michigan International Speedway	Brooklyn, Mich.	8	20	163/200	(mechanical)
Kentucky Speedway	Sparta, Ky.	1	16	184/200	
Pikes Peak International Raceway	Fountain, Colo.	5	8	223/225	
Infineon Raceway	Sonoma, Calif.	16	20	19/80	(accident)
Chicagoland Speedway	Joliet, Ill.	1	6	200/200	
Watkins Glen International	Watkins Glen, N.Y.	16	16	58/60	
California Speedway	Fontana, Calif.	4	18	184/200	(accident)

TOYOTA ATLANTIC SERIES—2004 >> Team: Team Rahal—Rahal Letterman Racing >> Car: Swift 014.a-Toyota 4A-GE

TRACK	LOCATION	START	FINISH	LAPS COMPLETED
Monterrey, Mexico	Street circuit	3	3	32/32
Long Beach, Calif.	Street circuit	6	5	31/31
The Milwaukee Mile	Milwaukee, Wisc.	6	4	70/70
Portland International Raceway	Portland, Ore.	3	2	35/35
Portland International Raceway	Portland, Ore.	1	7	35/35
Cleveland, Ohio	Airport circuit	8	3	32/32
Toronto, Canada	Street circuit	5	4	35/35
Vancouver, Canada	Street circuit	6	4	38/38
Road America	Elkhart Lake, Wisc.	6	4	17/17
Denver, Colo.	Street circuit	6	5	37/37
Circuit Gilles Villeneuve	Montreal, Canada	3	4	25/25
Laguna Seca Raceway	Monterey, Calif.	4	8	30/30

TOYOTA ATLANTIC SERIES—2003 >> Team: Team Rahal >> Car: Swift 014.a-Toyota 4A-GE

TRACK	LOCATION	START	FINISH	LAPS COMPLETED	
Monterrey, Mexico	Street circuit	5	3	32/32	
Long Beach, Calif.	Street circuit	10	14	19/32	(accident)
The Milwaukee Mile	Milwaukee, Wisc.	7	6	70/70	
Laguna Seca Raceway	Monterey, Calif.	9	13	0/30	(accident)
Portland International Raceway	Portland, Ore.	8	6	35/35	
Cleveland, Ohio	Airport circuit	10	5	32/32	
Toronto, Canada	Street circuit	9	10	35/35	
Trois-Rivieres, Canada	Street circuit	4	5	45/45	
Mid-Ohio Sport Car Course	Steam Corners, Ohio	11	10	30/30	
Circuit Gilles Villeneuve	Montreal, Canada	5	7	25/25	
Denver, Colo.	Street circuit	7	5	37/37	
Miami, Fla.	Street circuit	5	2	55/55	

1992
> Danica began karting at the age of 10 when her sister Brooke wanted to begin racing. Brooke abandoned the sport after a few months, but Danica was hooked.
> She was lapped six laps into her first event but finished the season second in the points championship out of 20 drivers.

1993
> In her second season of karting, she finished second in the WKA Midwest Sprint Series in both the Yamaha and US820 classes.
> She finished fourth in the WKA Manufacturer's Cup national points in the Yamaha Sportsman class.

1994
> At the age of 12, she captured her first national points championship in the WKA Manufacturer's Cup in the Yamaha Sportsman class.
> She won the WKA Great Lakes Sprint Series in the Yamaha Sportsman and US820 Sportsman classes.

1995
> Won the WKA Great Lakes Sprint Series title (Yamaha Restricted Junior and US 820 Jr.)
> Placed second in the WKA Manufacturer's Cup National Points titles in the same categories.

1996
> Established herself as a rising star in the karting ranks by winning 39 of 49 feature races (79.6%).
> At the age of 14, she won the WKA Manufacturer's Cup National Points title in the Yamaha Junior and Restricted Junior class.
> She was the runner-up in WKA Manufacturer's Cup National Points title (HPV 100 Junior) and the WKA Grand National Championship (Yamaha Restricted Junior).
> She captured five WKA Great Lakes Sprint Series and WKA Midwest Spring Series titles.
> She won the IKF Division 7 event in Willow Springs, California.
> (Yamaha Junior) and finished second in the IKF Grand Nationals in the Yamaha Junior group.

1997
> In her final full season of karting, she captured the World Karting Association (WKA) Grand National championship, HPV class.
> Won the WKA Grand National championship in Yamaha Lite class and won the WKA Summer National championship in Yamaha Lite class.
> Finished tenth in the Elk Constructors championship in Formula A.

1998
> Made her debut in England at age 16 in the Formula Vauxhall Winter Series.
> Ran a limited karting schedule while she attended the Formula Ford racing school in Canada.

1999
> Finished ninth in the Formula Vauxhall Championship in England, her first full season in the U.K.

2000
> Finished second at the Formula Ford Festival in England, the highest ever finish for an American.
> Drove for Andy Welch in the British Zetek Formula Ford Championship in England and for Haywood Racing in the European Formula Ford Series.
> Served as the lead test driver for Haywood Racing and Mygale Factory Team.

2001
> Competed in England, driving in the British Zetek Formula Ford Championship.
> Had successful test runs in USAC Midget, Toyota Atlantic, and ALMS cars.

2002—BARBER DODGE PRO SERIES
> Patrick signed a multi-year driving contract with Team Rahal.
> She was tabbed as the team's driver for a Toyota Atlantic entry in 2003.
> As preparation for her full-season effort in 2003, she ran a limited Barber-Dodge Pro Series schedule of five races.
> She made her debut at Toronto, qualifying eleventh and finishing seventh (7/7/02).
> Collected her highest finish of the Barber-Dodge Pro Series with a fourth-place finish at Vancouver (7/28/02).
> Tested a Busch Grand National car with PPC Racing in June.
> Captured the pole for the 2002 Long Beach Grand Prix Toyota Pro/Celebrity Race and won the pro division, topping former Trans Am champion Tommy Kendall and IRL driver Sarah Fisher.

INDEX